THE
DISTRIBUTED TEAMS
BLUEPRINT

Leveraging Remote Teams to Scale your Business

Adam Houlahan

AUTHOR OF AMAZON BESTSELLERS
The LinkedIn Playbook & Influencer

iX
indie\perts
PUBLISHING & AUTHOR SERVICES

First Published 2025

Published by Adam Houlahan

Produced by Indie Experts
www.indieexpertspublishing.com

Cover design and typesetting by Ammie Christiansen, Fast Forward Design
www.fastforwarddesign.co.nz
Typeset in 11.5pt Minion Pro

ISBN:
978-0-6453538-4-6 (Print)
978-0-6453538-5-3 (eBook)

Disclaimer:
Every effort has been made to ensure that this book is free from error or omissions. Information provided is of general nature only and should not be considered legal or financial advice. The intent is to offer a variety of information to the reader. However, the author, publisher, editor or their agents or representatives shall not accept responsibility for any loss or inconvenience caused to a person or organisation relying on this information.

Praise for *Distributed Teams Blueprint*

The level of detail here is stunning. It goes beyond classics like the E-Myth and pours on layer after layer of 'how-to's' that are absolutely stand out.

Destined to be a classic — get it and do it as soon as you can.

— PAUL DUNN

Co-Founder B1G1 | B1G1.com

'The Distributed Teams Blueprint' will save you a fortune and can even teach those of us who have been doing it for years some new tricks. Highly recommend this book!

— CALLUM LAING

Entrepreneur/Investor/Author | CallumLaing.com

A must-read for business leaders who want to grow globally and reduce their labour costs by leveraging high-calibre offshore talent.

— GAVIN LISTER

Lister Consulting | gavinlister.com

I wish this book had been written a couple of years ago. It would have saved me a lot of money and lost productivity.

Would give it 6 stars if I could!

— KARL SCHWANTES

Founder of Reputable
Author of Rock Her World | Reputable.global

Finally, a real-world, practical guide on how to scale results using remote teams, with proven, practical processes and protocols for scaling your results by looking after your team and supporting them.

My favourite part is The Buddy System because it acknowledges the power of diverse perspectives and demonstrates trust in Team Members.

— TOM POLAND

www.Leadsology.guru

From sourcing candidates, to selection, to contract negotiations, to onboarding, to communications, to managing your targeted and talented team of experts - this book is your one stop shop.

— KATE CHRISTIE

Time management expert
Best-selling author of The Life List

Think of this book as your step by step guide into the uncharted territory of distributed teams, pointing the way to seamless integration, innovation and performance.

— ROGER SIMPSON

CEO, The Retail Solution
Author of The Ultimate Retail Sales Experience

Distributed teams are part of the future, but leading distributed teams isn't easy. Adam's focus on the most important blocks of true team success helps navigate a huge challenge, and even bigger opportunity.

— BEN NASH

Author of: Get Unstuck; Replace Your Salary By Investing; Virgin Millionaire

Think of your team as the modern orchestra of business - each member playing their part harmoniously. This is especially true for distributed teams where each member, no matter how distant, adds their contribution to create a symphony of success.

Adam Houlahan doesn't just conduct, he hands you the sheet music, step-by-step, so your team can play with precision, alignment and excellence. This book isn't really about remote work - it's a master blueprint for building resilient, thriving teams that redefine what's possible in a hyper-connected, global marketplace.

— SIMON BOWEN

Founder The Models Method ©
Creator The Genius Model ©

What sets this book apart is its granular approach to remote leadership. It methodically walks through each phase of remote team management, offering concrete solutions rather than platitudes. From establishing virtual communication protocols to maintaining culture across time zones, the guidance is rooted in practical application.

I particularly appreciate how the content aligns with the realities of modern executive leadership. It's a valuable playbook that will serve as a go-to reference for any leader serious about building and scaling high-performing remote teams.

— DR. ANDRÉE BATES

CEO & Founder of Eularis

As a full-time digital nomad, I realise the power and benefits of building a remote team, Adam covers all the hurdles you might find and, most importantly, gives you a proven process to ensure success in building and leveraging a remote team.

— WAYNE SCHMIDT

Former country manager Xero
Current Digital Nomad

For full versions and more reviews please go to page 115.

THANK YOU FOR BEING PART OF THIS JOURNEY

I am deeply grateful that you've chosen to read The Distributed Teams Blueprint. This book is more than a guide—it's a labour of love, born out of the countless stories I've heard from organisations around the world. These stories, filled with gratitude for how we've helped them build thriving, connected teams, have been a profound source of inspiration for me. My hope is that the insights in these pages will ignite that same spark of transformation for you.

By purchasing this book, you've already taken a step that goes far beyond its contents. Through our partnership with the remarkable global initiative B1G1, your purchase has contributed to providing educational resources to underprivileged children. These textbooks open doors to opportunity—books that inspire young minds, tools that enable children to dream bigger, and knowledge that ripples out to families and communities. Together, we are sowing seeds of possibility and creating pathways to a brighter future.

I believe that true, lasting change begins with individuals like you—entrepreneurs and leaders who are breaking boundaries, connecting across cultures, and building teams that reflect the limitless potential of human collaboration. This book is designed to equip you with the strategies, tools, and vision to create distributed teams that not only excel but also contribute to the greater good.

This journey is one I'm honoured to share with you. My commitment to global giving is a cornerstone of my life's work, and through this shared mission, we have the opportunity to make a tangible difference together. Every team you build, every opportunity you create, is a step towards a more interconnected, equitable world.

I'll leave you with a favourite quote that captures the heart of this work: *"The strength of the team is each individual member. The strength of each member is the team."* —Phil Jackson

Here's to building teams that inspire, businesses that thrive, and a world that grows stronger—together.

Foreword

by Dr. David Dugan

Too many business owners exhaust themselves chasing growth, only to burn out. The difference between success and burnout isn't effort - it's strategy. This book unlocks the smarter, scalable way to achieve the business results you've always wanted.

Every now and then, a book comes along that not only informs but transforms how we think about business. This is one of those rare works.

I've known Adam for over a decade, and from the start, I was struck by his exceptional ability to uncover opportunities for true scaling—not just growing. Many business owners confuse growth with scale, but they're fundamentally different. Growth delivers linear returns, while scaling means for every effort there is a disproportionately higher return or exponential returns. This distinction is at the heart of Adam's work, and it's why I partnered with him in business.

Adam has an extraordinary ability to simplify complexity, making what seems overwhelming both understandable and actionable. This book is a great example of his genius. It's not just a collection of ideas; it's a step-by-step guide that empowers business owners to build elite, high-performing teams sourced globally. These teams often outperform local hires, all while being more affordable and quicker to assemble.

One of the most striking aspects of this book is how Adam codifies his proven strategies for success. He has applied these methods in his own ventures, including Prominence Global, where I'm a co-owner.

Inspired by his results, I've incorporated his approach across all my businesses, including my advisory firm, Abundance Global. The impact has been transformative.

Jim Collins, author of *Beyond Entrepreneurship 2.0,* identified that sustainable business success hinges on "the percentage of key seats filled by the right people." While this principle is widely accepted, it's often out of reach for small and medium-sized businesses due to the cost of hiring these talented people. Adam's book changes that. He provides a clear roadmap to fill those key seats affordably and effectively, unlocking the potential for sustainable scaling.

Adam's brilliance doesn't stop at his deep understanding of business. His passion for helping others succeed shines through every page. As a former CEO of a multinational company, he's mastered profitability while building loyal, high-performing teams.

To every business owner reading this, my advice is simple: study this book as if your business's future depends on it—because it might. Building and scaling a business isn't something you can do alone or with a small, stretched-thin team. Too many hardworking entrepreneurs burn under the weight of trying. But it doesn't have to be that way. This book gives you the tools, strategies, and clarity to succeed.

Act on these insights, and you'll gain the confidence to scale sustainably, build a self-sufficient business, and create the life and legacy you desire.

To every reader: the power to scale sustainably and profitably is within your reach. Your journey starts here.

Dr. David Dugan
BDSc, Adv Dip Bus, Grad Dip Clin Dent, Dip Fin Planning, Dip CH

Founder, Abundance Global Business Advisory

Contents

CHAPTER 1

The Distributed Teams Trend

The Working World Expands

In early 2023, it struck me that I no longer required an office that could house a team all based in the same city. I considered all the unused space and technology in my office and knew it was time to make some big decisions about the Prominence Global team structure. I was also becoming aware that many of our clients were being confronted by similar, related challenges: the difficulty of hiring talented people locally in the context of a growing skills shortage and *how* to transition to assembling great remote teams.

One of the commercial imperatives of the global pandemic was the need to revamp our attitude towards global and remote workforce opportunities.

This book was seeded by recognising that challenge and understanding my own advanced recruitment methods using LinkedIn. I've now got rid of that excess office space and replaced my old set-up with teams in India, the Philippines, Australia and Eastern Europe.

Now that it's possible for you to hire and manage remote team members by tapping into talent pools from all corners of the world, it's up to you to learn how to do this without making expensive and time-consuming mistakes. This book's purpose is to offer a simple explanation of the shifting landscape of attracting, recruiting and managing teams effectively, regardless of geographical boundaries.

Virtual Assistants, Diverse Teams, and Remote Contractors

Simply put, VAs provide businesses with a flexible and cost-effective way to handle various tasks without the need for physical office space. LinkedIn has become a vital platform for sourcing and managing VAs, especially from countries like the Philippines, where a large pool of skilled VAs is available.

The Shift to Diverse and Remote Work

This hasn't been a thing only since 2020. Even in the previous decade, the concept of remote work was evolving from being a niche practice to becoming a mainstream business strategy. Advances in communication technologies, cloud computing, and project management tools made it possible for team members to collaborate seamlessly from different locations. COVID accelerated an acceptance of people working from home offices, and many companies saw the value in downsizing from large corporate headquarters in favour of a more fluidly "onsite" team.

Companies like Prominence Global have leveraged these advancements to build successful remote teams. My expertise in LinkedIn strategies and my experience in digital entrepreneurship underscore the effectiveness of remote team models.

We no longer think only about remote VAs when we consider our need for extra help in our businesses now. And it's not only small businesses and entrepreneurs who rely on these external team members. "Diverse teams" and "remote teams" are now terms you'll hear commonly when referring to long-term company members.

What's the difference between diverse and remote?

One of the most surprising things about diverse teams and providers is that sometimes they are sitting right on your back doorstep. Under your very nose might be one, two, or ten people who can slot right into supplying you with what you need in your business for the time and tasks required, but they don't necessarily want to be employees.

Diverse team members want to be remote from your office. They might be digital nomads, serial entrepreneurs who prefer to work odd hours and pay their own taxes. They dictate what equipment and specialist knowledge they wish to work with, and it doesn't impact on you at all. They simply agree to a contract rate, do the work and get paid, and you get the results you need.

A remote team member is what we generally refer to as "overseas in some far-off land", such as the Philippines, China, or India. However, members of your entire business team are likely to be found in many more places than that.

Getting the Terminology Right

To make it easier to talk about remote teams, diverse teams and even virtual assistants across many industries, for the rest of this book we're going to talk about Distributed Teams. Everything we're going to lay out about building your own team of distributed workers will rely on your understanding of what they do, how they can work together as a high-functioning team, and what you can do to grow your business by embracing this exciting trend.

Currently, there are specialist providers of an enormous number of options – people working from many countries – and some have a reputation for specific specialties.

Several countries are renowned for their skillsets that a very adaptable to the distributed team concept, each excelling in different specialties:

THE PHILIPPINES

Specialty: Virtual assistants, customer support, and administrative tasks.

The Philippines is a popular source of virtual assistants and customer support roles. This is due to the country's strong English proficiency, cultural compatibility with Western countries, and a large pool of college-educated professionals.

INDIA

Specialty: IT and software development, customer service, and technical support.

India is well known for its IT and software development talent. The country also excels in providing customer service and technical support. Competitive costs and the large number of skilled professionals make India a preferred destination for these services.

UKRAINE

Specialty: Software development, IT services.

Ukraine has emerged as a hub for software development and IT services. The country is known for its highly skilled developers and cost-effective solutions.

POLAND

Specialty: IT services, engineering.

Poland is another significant player in the IT outsourcing market, providing high-quality IT services and engineering talent. The country benefits from a well-educated workforce and proximity to Western Europe.

MEXICO

Specialty: IT services, manufacturing support.

Mexico offers a growing pool of IT professionals and provides excellent support for manufacturing due to its proximity to the United States and NAFTA advantages.

VIETNAM

Specialty: Software development, IT services.

Vietnam is gaining recognition for its software development and IT services. The country offers a cost-effective alternative to more established markets like India and China.

BRAZIL

Specialty: IT services, creative design.

Brazil is known for its IT services and creative design talent, including graphic design and digital marketing. The country has a strong pool of skilled professionals and a growing tech industry.

BANGLADESH

Specialty: Data entry, administrative tasks, graphic design

Bangladesh provides services in data entry, administrative tasks, and graphic design. The country's growing focus on IT education is producing a skilled workforce suitable for various remote tasks.

ROMANIA

Specialty: IT services, engineering

Romania has a strong IT sector and is known for its engineering talent. The country benefits from a highly educated workforce and competitive costs.

ESTONIA

In 2020, Estonia became the first country in Europe to introduce Digital Nomad Visas. People working across a wide variety of specialist areas could base themselves there and work remotely on a global basis. Estonia's own citizens are also highly educated and the cost of living there is low enough compared with most other European countries to ensure competitive rates are available.

These countries have built strong reputations for their remote talent due to the availability of skilled labour, cost-effectiveness, and a conducive environment for remote work.

Digital Nomads base themselves in a variety of countries around the world. Some even work from yachts that are constantly sailing between locations. These people may be early retirees, or even young people who have decided to make full-time remote work their permanent lifestyle. Countries such as Estonia, Bali, Thailand, Greece, and Portugal have adjusted their entry visa requirements to accommodate these people.

Why not just employ locals who can do the job?

Let's say you need a new person to manage your website and social media and decide to recruit someone to work in-house. It's going to take time to find, interview, reference-check and onboard this one person. You'll need to provide them with a desk or office space, computer equipment, phone, probably also a camera or additional software to enable them to do the work required and ensure that they fit into the rest of your business. That person will be entitled to sick pay, holiday allowances, superannuation (currently an additional 11.5% of ordinary time earnings per team member, increasing to 12% in July 2025 in Australia). Workcover insurance increases with every new team member and can add tens of thousands in annual expenses. Ongoing training may be called for if they don't have all the skills you need. Your investment is likely to be upwards of approximately $100,000 – and that's to have just one highly skilled person for this role. Instead, you might find specialists with the skills you need residing in various parts of the world, and they already have the ability to work effectively as a team, unrestricted by their lack of ability to meet around the same table in real time.

You pay for what you need, when and how you need it, with specific contracts and clear mutual understanding of the KPIs required. A cost comparison for an in-house $100,000 team member against a distributed team member might require an investment 75%–40% less than that.

The Huge Benefits in Having a Global Team

1. **Access to a diverse talent pool:** By hiring remotely, businesses can access skills and expertise that might not be available locally. This diversity fosters innovation and brings different perspectives to problem-solving.
2. **Cost efficiency:** Remote teams can significantly reduce overhead costs associated with maintaining a physical office space. Additionally, hiring from regions with lower living costs can result in lower salary expenses without compromising on calibre of candidate.
3. **Flexibility and scalability:** Remote teams offer greater flexibility in scaling operations up or down based on business needs. This agility is particularly beneficial for startups and growing companies that need to adapt quickly to market changes.
4. **Increased productivity:** Studies have shown that remote team members often report higher productivity levels due to fewer distractions and a better work-life balance. Tools like video conferencing, collaborative software, and project management plat-

forms help maintain effective communication and coordination among team members.

5. **Global operations for any size business:** One of the biggest challenges in scaling an emerging enterprise is being able to service your clients in time zones outside your own. Many countries will be starting their day as your day ends. If you can't communicate with your clients during their normal office hours, the relationship will be short lived.

Challenges and Solutions

While the benefits are substantial, managing a remote team also presents challenges. These include issues related to communication, time zone differences, and maintaining company culture. However, with the right strategies, these challenges can be mitigated.

1. **Effective communication:** Using a mix of synchronous (video calls, chat) and asynchronous (emails, project management tools) communication methods can help bridge the gap. Regular check-ins and clear communication protocols are essential.

2. **Time zone management:** Scheduling tools and establishing core working hours that overlap for all team members can ensure timely collaboration. Flexibility and respect for different time zones is crucial.

3. **Building company culture:** Virtual team-building activities, regular virtual meetings, and fostering a sense of community through online platforms can help maintain and build company culture.

Remember this: the expansion into global and remote teams is not just a trend but a fundamental shift in how businesses operate. Working this way allows your company to be more resilient, adaptive, and competitive in today's market. Embracing this shift with effective strategies and tools will continue to unlock new potentials and drive business success in the digital age.

Another critical component of this working for businesses anywhere is that as we change our expectations about possibilities in terms of how to run a successful business, of any size, there is a mindset shift about the career paths of those on both sides of the equation.

Before we go any further…

What do you *think* you need in your business right now? Is it the same as you needed three or five years ago? What is the daily impact on your business of a more diverse and remote team?

By looking hard at what you have created so far, how you deliver your products and services to customers, and what their expectations are of you, you may immediately see how embracing a more diverse and remote team can help you plan growth. Ask yourself first, what really needs to be handled in-house? Does that in-house management need someone on a computer in an office in the next room – or in the next county?

Then, consider what could be possible. Is the service you provide in one country equally valuable to other countries around the world? Could you potentially expand the size of your market up to 10 times if you offered the same service you provide now to more countries?

The possibilities could seem incredibly exciting, and they are. But as a final exercise, ask yourself this question: if you don't expand your markets and build a highly efficient and cost-effective distributed team, how competitive will you remain when more of your current competitors do embrace this way of doing business? Similarly, how easily could your industry be disrupted by new players who do not have the legacy of high overheads in people, premises and oncosts that you currently consider a normal expense?

- Uber now provides the same service that taxis do, just more efficiently, with transparent pricing, real-time tracking of when your ride will arrive and reviews of your driver's history, to name a few.
- In the finance (banking) sector, fintechs such as PayPal and Stripe offer more flexible, faster, cheaper ways to transact globally than your bank used to.

When I launched Prominence Global in 2015, I liked the idea of having our team located in various locations because I was interested in getting a quality range of skills. We started out well, then decided to bring more of what we do to our central Gold Coast, Australia, location because of the perceived value in better collaboration being possible by having people working together, bouncing ideas around and exploring new opportunities together. The problem with that was the dramatically reduced number of candidates being offered to us. From an average talent pool of 50 or even hundreds to choose from, the recruitment agencies we partnered with would offer us fewer than five. That lack of selection showed us that the value we were aiming for was not possible.

In addition, because the people we wanted at Prominence Global had to be globally minded, early adopters and not tied to "regular office hours", we started to rethink how well we had already been operating. With the increased ability to engage well online and global acceptance of doing business differently through the pandemic era, it soon became apparent that our team had to become a distributed team. The advanced knowledge we have developed as a company regarding LinkedIn was already there. Moving to using LinkedIn became an easy decision to make.

You may already be engaging some distributed workers in your business; maybe you are still just thinking about these options. We need to explore what is possible and how this might impact on your specific operation. To help you further understand the scope of what's possible across *all* industry types, let's study some examples of specific skills and roles that people in distributed teams have.

CHAPTER 2

The Range of Roles Available

As I started writing this book, I began to compile a list of the roles that are options in a distributed team. This list has continued to grow, as I keep hearing about yet another company developing their distributed team with more and more roles that were traditionally in-house.

1. Accountants
2. Administrative assistants
3. Business development managers
4. Coaching
5. Compliance officers
6. Content creators
7. Content marketers
8. Copywriters
9. Customer service representatives
10. Data analysts
11. Digital marketing managers
12. e-Commerce managers
13. Editors
14. Email marketing specialists
15. Executive assistants
16. Financial analysts
17. Fundraising coordinators
18. Game designers
19. Graphic designers
20. Health and wellness coaches
21. HR managers
22. Insurance brokers

23. Instructional designers
24. Legal advisors
25. Marketing consultants
26. Medical coders
27. Mobile app developers
28. Online tutors
29. Operations managers
30. Payroll specialists
31. Podcast producers
32. Pay-per-Click (PPC) campaign managers
33. Project managers
34. Public relations specialists
35. Publishers
36. Quality assurance testers
37. Real estate agents (virtual)
38. Recruiters
39. Research analysts
40. Sales engineers
41. Sales representatives
42. SEO specialists
43. Social media managers
44. Software developers
45. System administrators
46. Technical support agents
47. Training and development specialists
48. Translators and interpreters
49. Travel agents
50. UX/UI designers
51. Video editors
52. Virtual assistants
53. Web developers

Let's consider further just what jobs can be done and the logistics of how they might fit into a company based in a Western country:

1. SOFTWARE DEVELOPMENT AND IT SUPPORT

- **Roles:** Software developers, web developers, mobile app developers, IT support specialists, system administrators.
- **Fit:** These roles are highly suitable for remote work as they require access to code repositories, collaboration tools, and communication platforms. Australasian companies can leverage global talent pools to access specialised skills or reduce costs.

For example: There's a popular online radio station in New Zealand which has their main studio based in Wellington, and one show host in the South Island and two in Auckland, each with their own independent studios. Their producers are based in either Wellington or Auckland, and their internet website and IT support team is based in Finland. The New Zealander who is head of IT travels back to New Zealand two or three times per year for some onsite meetings and planning requirements, but that is how the entire company is running and after two years is noted as a success story that is rapidly growing in strength.

2. DIGITAL MARKETING

- **Roles:** SEO specialists, content marketers, social media managers, email marketing specialists, PPC campaign managers.
- **Fit:** Digital marketing roles are ideal for remote work as they mainly involve online platforms and tools. Australasian companies can hire marketers from different time zones to ensure round-the-clock campaign monitoring.

For example: A Sydney-based SEO business decided to move into the fast-paced space of Voice Agents and other AI traffic generation technologies. As this is an emerging market, the availability of experienced and talented team members is very limited in Australia, let alone Sydney. The company decided to go global in their search for talent and have now built an exceptional distributed team across India, Nigeria and the Philippines for 80% per cent less than the cost of the annual salaries of their Australian counterparts.

3. FINANCE AND ACCOUNTING

- **Roles:** Accountants, bookkeepers, financial analysts, payroll specialists.
- **Fit:** These roles require secure access to financial software and data but can be performed from anywhere. Remote finance teams can help Western companies manage costs and handle compliance in multiple jurisdictions.

For example: Two Gold Coast-based accountants, who have known each other for many years, decided to join forces and open an office locally. Their combined client bases, and complementary areas of expertise makes this partnership a smart move. A couple of local team members are well supported by a Philippines-based team of bookkeepers fully acquainted with Australian accounting practices, and a marketing specialist in South Africa. They are on track for a 100% uplift in profitability in their first year.

4. CUSTOMER SUPPORT AND SERVICE

- **Roles:** Customer service representatives, technical support agents, virtual assistants.
- **Fit:** Customer support roles can be effectively outsourced or managed remotely, providing companies with the flexibility to offer 24/7 support. Australian companies can take advantage of time zone differences to provide after-hours support.

For example: A Brisbane-based law firm decided to do the reverse of the example of the accountants joining forces. After many years of working together, these two partners decided their passion for the law had grown in different specialties, and it made sense to split the firm into separate businesses focused in two different facets of law. One partner kept the existing structure, offices and team. The other took the opportunity to build a distributed team and has no offices, only two people employed in Australia and an offshore support team that meet the rest of their needs, including phone support, marketing and accounts payable/receivable across three different international locations.

5. HUMAN RESOURCES

- **Roles:** HR managers, recruiters, training and development specialists.
- **Fit:** HR tasks like recruitment, onboarding, and employee management can be managed remotely, allowing Australasian companies to access global talent pools and implement diverse training programs.

For example: A medium-sized company in Christchurch is engaging an entire distributed HR team to do their appointment setups, call backs and reference checks on candidates. The team is based in Manila, and a dedicated two-person team is assigned to their business. That duo also manages the onboarding paperwork, contracts, and employee reviews. The company used to have an in-house team but decided to start this distributed team option in 2024 after being approached by the Philippines service provider, whose language ability and communication skills are exceptional. They've even been able to request their duo work in a specific language and accents, and UK rather than US English is used for written communication.

6. GRAPHIC DESIGN AND CREATIVE SERVICES

- **Roles:** Graphic designers, video editors, copywriters, UX/UI designers.
- **Fit:** Creative roles are well suited to remote work due to the nature of the tasks which involve design software and communication tools. Australian companies can collaborate with international designers to bring diverse creative perspectives.

For example: My publisher's team is spread out globally with a website development and design team based between Hamilton in New Zealand and the Gold Coast in Australia. Their illustrator is in Auckland, the social media manager is in the Philippines, and the Chief Product Officer currently works between New Zealand, Bali and Europe. In 2024, they have worked with clients in Australia, New Zealand, the UK, the USA, South Africa and Sweden.

7. PROJECT MANAGEMENT

- **Roles:** Project managers, scrum masters, operations managers.
- **Fit:** Project managers can coordinate teams across different locations using collaboration tools like Slack, Trello, or Asana.

For example: A large dairy company in New Zealand is working with at least one of their distributed teams managing specific production factories around the country using Zoom and Teams for scheduled daily and weekly meetings. This started in 2020 but has moved from being a temporary work style to a permanent one. Each manager is required to be based in their regional offices two days per month; otherwise, they work from home, beach houses, or even on holiday internationally. They are achieving significant improvement in employee satisfaction and productivity.

8. SALES

- **Roles:** Sales representatives, account managers, business development managers.
- **Fit:** Sales roles, especially in B2B, can be handled remotely through video conferencing, CRM tools and online communication. Western-based companies can have sales teams in different markets to expand their reach.

For example: A UK-based SAAS provider has built their distributed team throughout Eastern European countries at a fraction of the cost for equally skilled team members in the UK. The affordability of their new team has allowed them to triple their outbound sales efforts, resulting in more than a 400% increase in profit after releasing an updated version of a popular product they have been supplying for the last 11 years.

9. LEGAL AND FINANCIAL SERVICES

- **Roles:** Legal advisors, contract managers, compliance officers.
- **Fit:** Legal professionals can work remotely on tasks like contract review, compliance checks and legal research. Australasian professional services companies can use administration and copywriting skills from a variety of places to manage international legal matters.

For example: A small family insurance and financial planning company based in New Zealand wanted to stay small in terms of office space and to keep a family feel for their company. When they identified a need for specialist help with spreadsheets, coding, and some specific administration tasks, they decided to look beyond the option of expanding their in-house capacity. They now have, on contract, a woman in California who works 10 hours per week for them, providing her own office facilities and charging a rate that is only a little higher than they would pay per hour for someone in-house. The company feels getting a globally focused range of skills for a part-time role is better for their business than accommodating that role locally. And as their clients also become more mobile in their work, the company is now well equipped to manage global expectations, even on a relatively small scale.

10. PROPERTY AND INVESTMENT SERVICES

- **Roles:** Real estate analyst, leasing agent, marketing specialist.
- **Fit:** These roles support the various facets of property investment, from marketing for both investors and sellers and identifying new opportunities to managing existing assets and ensuring legal and financial compliance.

For example: A Sydney-based property coaching and investment organisation has built an exceptional team with a blend of local and international talent. Being well known for their in-person seminars in Sydney, they decided to expand their reach by hosting online web events to complement their live events. They have team members in the Philippines managing customer service and support duties, as well as a marketing team based in South Africa.

11. INSURANCE AND MORTGAGE BROKERAGE

- **Roles:** Account manager, claims agent, marketing specialist, customer service.
- **Fit:** These roles form an interconnected system that handles every aspect of an insurance or mortgage brokerage business – from client acquisition and relationship management to compliance, operations and financial sustainability.

For example: A Melbourne-based mortgage broker decided to acquire a Brisbane-based brokerage to expand their client base and revenue. An unforeseen challenge that arose turned out to be a massive opportunity. The existing team that came with the acquired business were very used to how the business operated under the original management and resisted the changes the new owners wanted to implement. One by one, the old team left the business. The decision was made to replace most of these roles with distributed team members offshore and expand the roles of existing team members in Melbourne, who were fully onboard with the way they operated. Some foresight was applied by the new owners, who started recruiting and training the offshore team ahead of the resignations through the Melbourne office, which ensured minimal disruption in the changeover.

12. VIRTUAL ASSISTANT AGENCIES

- **Roles:** Choose any of those listed above
- **Fit:** There is a growing business model of companies hiring their

own distributed team members and offering services to you on a permanent or subscription type system. The rates are understandably higher than having these team members as a permanent part of your team, but can give you access to a diversity of skills and flexibility when your need for these people is only temporary.

For example: A US-based company has rented buildings in Manila and has hired team members who can perform over 30 different tasks their North American clients need access to and offer these services on a subscription model. Depending on the volume of workload their clients require, they have different packages at a fixed monthly fee. This allows their clients to access these skills without needing a fulltime person in each role, which is perfect for many growing businesses. They have locally based account managers in the US who liaise with team captains in Manila to maintain a cohesive workflow delivery.

By effectively managing communication, collaboration and time zone differences, Australasian, North American and European companies can easily build robust and efficient distributed teams that contribute to their overall success.

How it works for a retailer

If we look at even just one industry to analyse the many ways a distributed team can be a good fit, then perhaps we should start with a retail company. Traditionally, a retailer needed people to be in one location, but that is not the case anymore. Online sales and marketing portals, customer services, and all that goes into making a retail experience both online and instore can easily be enhanced utilising a distributed team. In fact, as many as 10 roles within retail can effectively be filled by remote team members, from as far away as the other side of the world.

1. E-COMMERCE PLATFORM DEVELOPMENT

- **Scenario:** A retail company wants to expand its business by launching an online store.

- **Enhancement:** Software developers can create a customised e-commerce platform that integrates seamlessly with the retailer's existing inventory system. This platform would offer features like product search, secure payment gateways, customer reviews, and personalised recommendations. With a robust online presence, the retailer can reach a wider audience, increase sales, and offer customers a convenient shopping experience.

2. MOBILE APPLICATION DEVELOPMENT

- **Scenario:** The retailer wants to enhance customer engagement and loyalty through a mobile app.

- **Enhancement:** Software developers can build a mobile app that provides features such as in-app purchases, loyalty programs, push notifications for promotions, and location-based services to guide customers to the nearest store. The app can also include augmented reality features for virtual try-ons or product previews. This enhances customer interaction, drives repeat business, and boosts brand loyalty.

3. INVENTORY MANAGEMENT SYSTEM

- **Scenario:** The retailer struggles with managing inventory across multiple stores and warehouses.

- **Enhancement:** IT support and software development teams can implement an inventory management system that provides real-time tracking of stock levels, automatic reordering of popular items, and integration with the sales data to predict future demand. This system would reduce the likelihood of stockouts or overstocking, optimise storage costs, and improve overall operational efficiency.

4. CUSTOMER RELATIONSHIP MANAGEMENT (CRM) SYSTEM

- **Scenario:** The retailer wants to improve customer service and personalise marketing efforts.

- **Enhancement:** A software development team can develop a CRM system allows the retailer to store and analyse customer data, track purchase histories, and segment customers for targeted marketing campaigns. IT support ensures the system runs smoothly, helping the retailer deliver personalised offers, improve customer retention, and increase sales.

5. CYBERSECURITY SOLUTIONS

- **Scenario:** The retailer is concerned about protecting customer data and preventing breaches.

- **Enhancement:** IT support specialists can implement advanced cybersecurity measures, including encryption, multi-factor authentication, and regular security audits. Software developers can also build secure checkout processes for online transactions and monitor systems for potential threats. These measures help protect the retailer from data breaches, maintain customer trust, and ensure compliance with data protection regulations.

6. POINT-OF-SALE (POS) SYSTEM UPGRADE

- **Scenario:** The retailer uses slow, outdated POS systems that lack modern features.

- **Enhancement:** Software developers can design and deploy a modern POS system with features like mobile payments, digital receipts, and integration with the retailer's CRM and inventory management systems. IT support ensures that these systems are always up and running, reducing downtime and improving the customer checkout experience. This leads to faster transactions, better data collection, and enhanced customer service.

7. DATA ANALYTICS AND BUSINESS INTELLIGENCE

- **Scenario:** The retailer wants to make data-driven decisions to optimise sales and operations.
- **Enhancement:** Software developers can create data analytics tools that collect and analyse sales, customer behaviour, and market trends. IT support teams maintain the infrastructure required for these tools to operate efficiently. By leveraging these insights, the retailer can optimise pricing strategies, identify popular products, and tailor marketing campaigns to boost profitability.

8. CLOUD-BASED SOLUTIONS

- **Scenario:** The retailer needs to scale its IT infrastructure to support business growth.
- **Enhancement:** IT support teams can migrate the retailer's operations to cloud-based solutions, enabling greater scalability, flexibility, and cost efficiency. Software developers can build cloud-native applications that enhance collaboration, data storage, and customer service capabilities. This transition to the cloud allows the retailer to handle increased traffic, improve disaster recovery, and reduce IT costs.

9. AUTOMATED CUSTOMER SUPPORT

- **Scenario:** The retailer wants to improve customer support without significantly increasing staffing costs.
- **Enhancement:** Software developers can create chatbots and AI-driven customer support systems that handle common enquiries, track orders, and provide 24/7 assistance. IT support ensures these systems are integrated with the retailer's CRM and other support tools. This automation enhances customer satisfaction by providing quick responses and frees up human agents to handle more complex issues.

10. OMNICHANNEL RETAIL INTEGRATION

- **Scenario:** The retailer wants to offer a seamless shopping experience across online and offline channels.

- **Enhancement:** Software developers can build an omnichannel platform that synchronises the retailer's website, mobile app, and physical stores. This system allows customers to browse products online and pick them up in-store or return items purchased online at a physical location. IT support ensures the seamless integration of these channels, providing a consistent and convenient shopping experience that boosts customer satisfaction and loyalty.

This selection of roles clearly illustrates how software development and IT support can significantly enhance a retailer's operations, improve customer experiences, and drive business growth in a competitive market. If retailers can do this, imagine how any other industry might also be able to use distributed teams for a wide variety of operational work. Let's face it, the world of consumerism, creativity, management, and operations is changing. So now let's look at some of the thinking that has to be applied to make it work.

CHAPTER 3

Employee vs Contractor

Navigating the landscape of remote work requires a robust framework to ensure success and compliance. One of the foundational elements of this framework is the service contract, in contrast to an employment contract. A well-crafted service contract sets clear expectations and provides a legal safeguard for both parties. As someone deeply involved in the realm of digital strategy and entrepreneurship, I understand the transformative power of clear agreements. Over the years, through my journey from launching my first book *Social Media Secret Sauce* to establishing our LinkedIn Personal Brand and Lead Generation agency Prominence Global, I've seen firsthand the critical role that structured, transparent contracts play in fostering effective remote teams.

In working with entrepreneurs globally, including hosting one of the largest free online LinkedIn training events with over 15,000 registrants annually, I emphasise the impact of preparation and clarity. Just as a detailed LinkedIn profile can impact professional connections and opportunities, a comprehensive service contract is vital for building a successful remote workforce.

First, let's get clear on the difference between employees (who may or may not work remotely) and contractors (who also may or may not work remotely). Your ideal option with distributed teams is to have contractors who are self-employed work under an established agreement and who provide their own resources to do the work you need them to do. They are likely to have their own phones, offices, computers, software, etc. Their reporting process is going to be based on what you require, and you will set their KPIs at the beginning of your term.

This will most likely require a small shift in your thinking about people working in your company. These people, if successfully working remotely already, are already proven self-starters and self-managing high achievers.

The following grid will help you to adjust this thinking

EMPLOYEE	CONTRACTOR
• Comes to work at a designated place of employment. • Tools for the job are typically provided unless you are a chef or tradesperson who is encouraged to invest in their own tools of trade. • Lunchbreaks, start and end times, and holidays are all predetermined, and times are built into their job description. • A union or industry association might dictate some of those benefits, like regular breaks, pay rises, salary levels, holidays, and sick pay.	• Might work from anywhere in the world. • Provides their own computer, internet, phone, and training, and will invest in their skill sets and capabilities in order to attract the best contracts. • Contractors will be paid according to their delivery of KPIs and tasks as per their contracted agreement. They are responsible for their own taxes but still work within set hours that suit you, which may or may not be within the hours you normally operate your business.

• An employee has rights, often enforced by the courts of the land, to be treated a certain way. These rights relate to but are not limited to discrimination, training, and termination of employment.	• A contractor has rights according to the agreement they sign with you, as do you.
• An employer may have rights to have expectations of certain behaviour even outside their employees' place of business; i.e., industry moral codes for professionals and tradespeople.	• A contracted member of a distributed team is reliant on their reputation for good delivery, standards and abilities.
• An employee might have rights to superannuation or health insurance benefits provided by the company.	• The contracted member might be required to have certain insurances in place.*

*Insurance for some contractors might include professional indemnity to cover any wrongdoing, or misunderstandings, or accidental breaches of confidence leading to adverse implications for their clients – i.e., *you*. It is always worth asking a potential contracted team member if they have this. It may vary depending on your industry type and the country they are based in.

There are, of course, some exceptions to all these instances; for example, a contracted distributed team member might be expected to have certain qualifications or industry memberships to support their work. They may also be required to sign non-disclosure agreements, or make it known what other contracts they are working with if there are any perceived conflicts of interest, but this gets worked out and resolved through the process of engagement.

Drafting Contracts

When drafting contracts for remote team members, several key elements must be included:

1. **ROLES AND RESPONSIBILITIES:** Clearly define your expectations of the contracted person. This includes specific duties, reporting lines, and performance expectations.

2. **COMPENSATION AND BENEFITS:** Detail the payment levels and schedule of payments, and any additional benefits (if there are any) of being engaged with your company. This might include bonuses, insurances, and training incentives.

3. **WORKING HOURS AND FLEXIBILITY:** Outline the expected working hours. If your team spans multiple time zones, specify core hours when all team members should be available.

4. **TERMINATION CONDITIONS:** Define the terms under which the contract can be terminated by either party. Include notice periods and any severance arrangements.

5. **INTELLECTUAL PROPERTY AND CONFIDENTIALITY:** Include clauses that protect your company's intellectual property and ensure confidentiality. This is especially important for remote workers who may have access to sensitive information from various locations.

Next Steps

1. **DRAFT THE CONTRACT:** Use the information outlined above to draft out a contract that will be workable and robust for your company based on the industry you are in and the work required.

2. **LEGAL REVIEW:** Schedule a review with a legal expert to ensure compliance and accuracy of the contract.

3. **FINALISE:** Make any necessary adjustments based on the legal advice.

4. **ONBOARD:** Present and explain the contract to the new hire, ensuring mutual understanding and agreement.

5. By establishing a clear foundation of expectations and responsibilities, a solid contract fosters a trustworthy and professional working relationship from the very start.

6. If you are going to add contracted distributed team members, there are things you need to think about, prepare for and discuss with your existing stakeholders. A lot could go wrong with this, but a lot more can go right, once you have progressed through the planning and preparation stages appropriately.

7. It's a good idea to spend time talking with others in your network who have engaged remote team members. And if you need professional assistance in working through the process of finding and engaging great people, my company, Prominence Global, can assist you. There are some options listed for how we can guide, assist and serve you in this area on page 109.

8. Now that we've established what kind of roles might be filled by distributed teams and the difference between employee and contractors, it's time to think through what you need.

9. A detailed checklist will ensure all critical steps are covered. Here's an example that provides a structured approach to engaging and onboarding remote contractors, ensuring that both the company and the contractor have clear expectations and are set up for success.

Distributed Teams Contractor Engagement Checklist

First, decide *how* you wish to engage someone. Will you go online yourself, or engage the help of a professional HR or industry expert?

1. PRE-CONTRACTUAL DUE DILIGENCE

- **Identify exactly what you need, and the roles, skills and certifications required**:
    - Define the specific tasks and responsibilities required for the role.
    - Assess whether the contractor needs specialised skills or certifications.
- **Legal compliance:**
    - Understand the legal implications of your service contract and its enforceability.
    - Verify the contractor's ability to work (e.g., business licenses, right to work in their country).
    - Consult with legal and/or HR experts to draft a compliant contract.
- **Background checks:**
    - Perform background checks, including references and previous work assessments.
        - Who have they worked with before that you can recognise (by industry type or recommendations)?

- ◆ If applicable, what "star rating" have they got?
- ◆ Where do they work from – in what time zones/languages?
- ◆ Can they show you samples of work – designs, written, produced goods?

- **Contract drafting:**
  - ▪ Draft a comprehensive contract outlining roles, responsibilities, KPIs, compensation, and termination conditions.
    - ◆ What will you pay them? Will it be monthly, weekly, or at other intervals?
    - ◆ What will you do if you are unhappy with their work?
    - ◆ How do you propose to manage their KPIs?
  - ▪ Include clauses on intellectual property, confidentiality, and non-compete agreements, where relevant.

2. TECHNOLOGY AND EQUIPMENT SET-UP

- **Technology requirements:**
  - ▪ Specify required technology tools and platforms (e.g., project management tools, communication platforms) you require them to have, know, and use vs what you will provide for them.
    - ◆ Include specific software knowledge and use competence, such as Zoom vs Teams for meetings; Dropbox vs Google Docs for sharing files; Canva vs Adobe Photoshop for design; Xero vs MYOB for accounting and administration.
  - ▪ Confirm the contractor has the necessary equipment (e.g., computers, software, internet access).
    - ◆ You may need to specify and confirm reliable internet access and speed.

- **Security and compliance:**
  - Ensure data protection measures are in place, including secure access to company systems.
    - This is also a good time to review your internal cyber security measures.
  - Provide necessary cybersecurity training if needed.

3. COMMUNICATION AND COLLABORATION TOOLS

- **Tool access:**
  - Provide access to necessary communication tools (e.g., Slack, Zoom, Teams, WhatsApp).
  - Set up accounts for project management and time-tracking software.
- **Training on tools:**
  - Schedule training sessions for the contractor on how to use company-specific tools and software.
- **Establish communication protocols:**
  - Define communication channels and expectations (e.g., response times, preferred communication methods).
  - Define your preferred schedule of check-ins, meetings, delivery of updates and completion of projects.

4. ONBOARDING AND ORIENTATION

- **Welcome and introduction:**
  - Arrange virtual introductions to key team members and stakeholders.
  - Send a welcome kit, including a description of company values and culture, and necessary onboarding materials.
    - Do you already have these or do you need to develop induction tools for your company? Does what you

have work for remote workers?

- **Orientation:**
  - Provide an overview of the company's mission, vision and work culture.
  - Outline expectations for performance and key deliverables during the first 90 days.

5. PERFORMANCE AND ACCOUNTABILITY

- **Define key performance indicators (KPIs):**
  - Clearly outline KPIs and the metrics by which performance will be evaluated.
  - Establish a feedback mechanism for continuous improvement and communication.
- **Monitoring and reporting:**
  - Set up regular reporting schedules to track progress on deliverables.
  - Use project management tools to monitor ongoing tasks and project statuses.

6. FINAL CONTRACTUAL AGREEMENT

- **Review and finalise contract:**
  - Conduct a final review of the contract with legal advisors.
  - Make any necessary adjustments based on feedback.
  - Get the contractor's agreement and signature on the finalised contract.
- **Insurance and risk management:**
  - Confirm if the contractor requires any specific insurance (e.g., professional indemnity)

7. POST-ENGAGEMENT REVIEW

- **Performance review:**
  - After the first major deliverable, review the contractor's performance against KPIs.
  - Provide feedback and make necessary adjustments to the work process.

- **Continuous improvement:**
  - Collect feedback from the contractor regarding the engagement process to improve future contractor onboarding.
  - Your objective here is to consider how you will develop a positive working relationship with members of your distributed teams. Just because they are not working in your physical space does not preclude you from having an ongoing connection as they contribute to the success of your projects and your business as a whole.

As you work through this checklist, you will also need to consider what you already have in place, such as values and mission statements and clearly defined team-building and induction processes.

It is worth repeating that the decision to engage distributed teams as an option for sustainable growth and development of your business is not to be taken lightly. The more planning and forethought you engage in at the start, the better the results will be for your business in the long run.

* Prominence Global has an exceptional Distributed Team with expertise in helping companies to engage in this process. Please check the options on page 109 if you need help.

CHAPTER 4

Crafting the Perfect Welcome Kit

The first day for any new team member sets the tone for the rest of their experience with your company, and when it comes to distributed teams, this first impression is even more important. Without the luxury of face-to-face interaction, companies need to be creative in establishing connection and making new members feel welcomed and integrated. One way to achieve this is through a thoughtfully curated **welcome kit**. A welcome kit not only introduces the company culture but also provides practical tools and a warm, personal touch that can reduce the initial distance your remote team might feel.

Here's what you need to include to get the right message and tone to welcome your newest recruit and how the kit can be an extension of your company culture.

The Role of a Welcome Kit in Remote Onboarding

While the core of a successful onboarding program includes clear communication, a comprehensive training plan, and a roadmap for success, the **welcome kit** serves as the tangible element that brings everything together. For people who are not physically present in an office, receiving a package (either by physical mail or email) ahead of their start date can make a world of difference.

A personalised welcome kit achieves several goals:

1. **Setting the tone**: It acts as the first official gesture from your company signalling that their presence is valued and that the company is prepared to support them.

2. **Communicating culture**: The contents of the kit should reflect the company's culture and values, helping your new team members feel like part of the team from day one.

3. **Practical preparation**: A physical welcome kit can include essential items like tech equipment, branded merchandise, and company documents. If sending an email is the only option, personalised documentation, a warm welcoming letter that is personalised and other connection points can also help with the set-up process.

Whether you send a physical package or not at the start will come down to your new person's location, ease of sending, and perhaps the length of contract. A two-phase option might work for you, such as starting with the digital package, followed up later by the physical package. You'll want to aim for a combination of practical tools and personal touches. Below are some key items to consider including:

1. Branded items

A welcome kit should have a few branded items that reflect your company's identity. These can include:

- **Notebooks and pens:** Simple but useful, branded stationery serves as both a practical tool and a daily reminder of your company's presence.

- **Coffee mugs or water bottles:** Items like mugs or water bottles are functional and commonly used during work hours. With your logo on them, they become small reminders of belonging.

- **T-shirts, hoodies, or hats:** Clothing items that feature your company logo give new employees a sense of identity and affiliation with the brand.

Branded items aren't just for marketing – they help create a visual link between the employee and the company, fostering a sense of connection even from a distance.

2. A personal welcome letter

A handwritten welcome note from the CEO, the direct manager, or the HR team can make a significant impact. In this letter, you can:

- Express excitement about having the new team member onboard.
- Highlight key aspects of the company culture that the new person should be excited about.
- Provide a personal anecdote or motivation behind the company's mission to create a more meaningful connection.

Personalisation is key here. Mentioning the new person's name and a specific detail about their role or the hiring process can make this gesture feel more genuine.

3. Onboarding schedule and information

New people might feel overwhelmed by all the information they need to absorb. Including a printed onboarding schedule in the kit helps them visualise their first few weeks and sets expectations. Along with the schedule, include:

- A **company handbook** that outlines your mission, values, and policies.
- A **team directory** that includes short bios or fun facts about key team members they will be working with.

- **Log-in details** for any communication platforms (like Slack, Microsoft Teams) or project management tools (like Asana, Trello) they will be using.

Providing this information ahead of time helps smooth the transition and minimises first-day jitters.

4. Essential tools for success

Your distributed teams are likely to supply their own laptops and general equipment, but there may be other things you can send to make their roles and transition to becoming a valued team member easier. You might want to also include smaller, essential tools within the welcome kit:

- **USB drives** pre-loaded with essential software or documents.
- **A mouse pad** with a motivational quote or company slogan.
- **Cable organisers** to help the new person keep their workspace tidy.

These items are small but thoughtful additions that can enhance their productivity from the start.

How far you wish to progress along these lines depends on your terms of engagement, what the new distributed team member is required to do, and how involved they are required to be.

Personalisation: The key to connection

The most memorable welcome kits go beyond branded swag and office supplies; they add personal touches that show genuine care for the team member. Consider including:

- **A book** that aligns with the company's culture or industry. For instance, if your company values leadership, include a popular business book like *Leaders Eat Last: Why Some Teams Pull Together and Others Don't* by Simon Sinek (Penguin Books, 2000).

Adding a note about why this book is relevant to the company can make the gesture even more thoughtful.

- Why not make a list of all the great articles, book links, and resources you like to share with your teams, and add these to a complete welcome page section of your website – then send a physical version of a book you want to share directly from Amazon or IngramSpark, with a customised note inside.

The Logistics of Sending a Welcome Kit

Logistics are crucial when delivering welcome kits, especially for distributed team members who are long-term hires. Ensure that the kit arrives **before** the new person's start date. Ideally, the new hire should receive it a few days in advance, giving them time to explore the contents and feel excited for their first day.

If your team is spread across different countries or continents, work with a logistics provider that offers **international shipping.** Also, consider packaging that is both sturdy and aesthetically pleasing, adding to the unboxing experience.

Ensure you have all the information you need to progress with the onboarding.

You'll require them to confirm such information as:

- Full name, address, contact information
- Payment details
- Zoom, Dropbox, Trello, LastPass, LinkedIn and social media presence, and industry-specific software set.
- Email address for your communications: I recommend you set medium- and long-term contracts up with an email address inside your own company, so that if you need to access their communications you can, and that if you have to let them go

at any time, you can retain all the information relevant to your business.

First Day Essentials

Introductions: Building Connections on Day One

Since remote team members miss out on the face-to-face interactions that naturally occur in an office setting, companies need to be intentional about fostering relationships and making the new hire feel like a part of the team. A well-executed **introduction process** on the first day sets the stage for long-term collaboration, trust, and a positive work culture.

1. Virtual welcome meeting

The first step in welcoming your new person is scheduling a **virtual welcome meeting** with the entire team. This gives the new hire a broader sense of who they will be working with and creates a shared sense of excitement.

Here are a few tips to make the virtual welcome meeting impactful:

- **Keep it informal**: Start with light conversations to ease any nerves. Encourage the team to introduce themselves briefly, perhaps sharing their role and a fun fact about themselves.
- **Highlight the new hire**: Give the new person the opportunity to introduce themselves and share a bit about their background, interests, and what excites them about joining the company.
- **Team overview**: Include a brief overview of the team's current projects and goals. This will provide context for how the new addition will fit into the team's broader objectives.

2. Introducing key players

After the team welcome, the new hire should meet the people they will be directly working with. This typically includes the **direct manager**, **assigned buddy**, and **key team members**.

- **Direct manager introduction**: This one-on-one conversation sets the tone for the new team member-manager relationship. It's a good opportunity to discuss immediate priorities, upcoming projects, and the team culture. The manager should also use this time to reassure the new hire that they are there for support.
- **Assigned buddy**: A buddy system is particularly effective in remote teams. The buddy, ideally someone from another department, provides insight into the company culture and can answer questions that might not be as easily addressed by the manager. This relationship helps the new hire feel more connected across the company.

3. One-on-one meetings for in-depth introductions

To further integrate the new hire into the team, schedule **one-on-one meetings** with team members they will collaborate with regularly. These deeper, personal interactions allow the employee to:

- build rapport on an individual level
- understand specific team dynamics and expectations
- learn about each team member's role and how their work will overlap.

These meetings should be spread out over the first week to avoid overwhelming the new hire, but ensure they happen early to encourage swift integration.

Ideally, have the buddy assigned to the new hire check in with them for a friendly conversation to ensure that all has been taken care of and expectations are being met at the end of that first week. This also helps the new person to better connect with that buddy and for any early troubleshooting if there's a need.

CHAPTER 5

Navigating Global Time Zones, Public Holidays, Communication

Managing a distributed team that spans different time zones, countries, and cultures presents unique challenges, such as coordinating communication across multiple time zones and navigating regional public holidays without disrupting the workflow. As organisations increasingly rely on remotely located people, managing these logistical hurdles is key to maintaining productivity and team cohesion.

One company I work with has their team of six people located in six countries and seven times zones. The time zone differences look like this:

While in WA the time is ↓	WA	WA	WA
Western Australia	12 noon	7 am	9 pm
Queensland, Australia	2 pm	9 am	11 pm
Bali, Indonesia	12 noon	7 am	9 pm
Manila, the Philippines	12 noon	7 am	9 pm
New Zealand	4 pm	11 am	1 am
Texas, USA	11 pm	6 pm	8 am
Spain	6 am	1 am	3 pm

Can you imagine the extra headache of trying to get meetings to work for everyone if the company decided to add another person based in Europe? Does this kind of situation have an impact on deciding who to engage as new distributed team members? Well, that depends on many things, such as which parts of the teams need to be conversant with each other and how much time lag the roles allow for.

Effective global coordination requires a balance between flexibility and structure. Teams need the right strategies and tools to communicate clearly, keep projects on track, and respect individual time zones and cultural holidays. But you can develop some key strategies to manage time zone differences, public holidays, and communication within distributed teams.

Managing Global Time Zones

Time zone differences are a common challenge for distributed teams. Without proper strategies in place, teams can experience delays in communication, missed meetings, or a breakdown in collaboration. Here's how to navigate these challenges with ease.

Flexible Scheduling

Traditional 9-to-5 workdays may not apply when your team spans multiple continents, so allowing people to adjust their schedules can lead to better work-life balance and productivity. Flexibility enables team members in different regions to collaborate during overlapping hours, which is crucial for synchronous tasks such as meetings or brainstorming sessions.

It might also suit some people more to work at night, or very early in the morning, rather than during traditional daytime hours. If someone has other international contracts, then as a distributed team member they may choose to regularly start their day at 4 am, work for a few hours, then surf or study or do whatever else they like from midday onwards. You get the idea.

Tools like World Time Buddy or Google Calendar can be invaluable when coordinating across time zones. These scheduling tools help identify overlapping hours when the *majority* of the team can connect. This makes it easier to plan meetings or deadlines while considering the working hours of all team members. For example, if you have people in the US, Europe, and Asia, using a tool like World Time Buddy can help pinpoint windows of time when everyone is available, even if it's just for a short meeting.

Core Working Hours

While flexible hours are important, it's also crucial to establish core working hours – specific blocks of time when most, if not all, team members are expected to be available. This ensures there are periods during the day where direct communication can take place, helping to streamline decision-making and team collaboration. Core working hours serve as an anchor point for scheduling meetings and handling urgent matters, ensuring that no one feels left out or isolated due to time zone differences.

However, depending on the geographical spread of the team, achieving a universally convenient time for everyone may be impossible. In such cases, it's important to prioritise flexibility and encourage asynchronous communication, allowing those in different time zones to contribute on their own schedules.

Asynchronous Communication

When it is simply unrealistic for everyone to be available at the same time, then you need to rely on asynchronous communication. Tools like Trello, Asana, and Slack are designed to support asynchronous collaboration, allowing team members to share updates, leave feedback, and track progress without really needing real-time interaction.

Asynchronous communication is especially useful for tasks that do not require immediate responses, such as writing reports, coding, or designing. By leveraging project management tools, team members can assign tasks, provide updates, and comment on progress at times that work best for them. This allows the team to move forward even when some members are offline.

Another key benefit of prepared asynchronous communication is that it reduces the pressure for immediate replies, which can often lead to burnout in remote teams. By preferring thoughtful, well-considered responses over rushed, real-time interactions, teams can improve both the quality of their work and overall communication.

Rotating Meeting Times

While asynchronous communication is essential, there may still be those times when live meetings are necessary. To ensure no team member is consistently inconvenienced, rotating meeting times is an effective strategy. For example, if a weekly meeting is scheduled at 9 am US Eastern Time, which is 10 pm in the Philippines (depending on daylight saving protocols), the following week's meeting could be held at a time more convenient for team members in Australia or Europe.

Rotating meeting times not only demonstrates respect for the team's diversity, but it also helps distribute the inconvenience of working outside standard hours. This approach fosters a more inclusive work culture and ensures that no single group is consistently disadvantaged by time zone differences. Flexibility and a willingness to work through the challenges is what will make it succeed.

CHAPTER 6

Navigating Public Holidays in Distributed Teams

Public holidays pose another logistical challenge in distributed teams. A holiday in one country often means a regular workday for team members in another, which can disrupt project timelines and communication. Successfully managing public holidays in distributed teams requires thoughtful planning and flexibility.

Understanding Regional Holidays

The first step is recognising the regional holidays observed by your team members. For example, team members in India may observe Diwali, while those in the Philippines may take time off for Holy Week. Knowing these dates in advance allows managers to plan around them and avoid scheduling important meetings or deadlines during those times.

Daylight saving may also mean a few additional challenges. I know one New Zealand-based company that sets all their times for meetings with clients and team members based on Queensland Australia times, because that is unchanging. Queensland does not impose daylight saving, while various other parts of the world do, and the company has found that having at least *one* fixed time throughout the year makes global meetings and collaborations much easier for all involved.

Creating a Shared Holiday and Time Zones Calendar

A shared holiday calendar that includes the public holidays of all team members is an essential tool for distributed teams. Platforms like Google Calendar or Microsoft Outlook allow you to create a consolidated holiday/zones calendar, which can be shared with the entire team. This way, everyone knows when certain team members will be unavailable, helping to prevent last-minute surprises or missed deadlines.

Offering Flexible Holiday Policies

To accommodate the diversity of public holidays, companies can offer flexible holiday policies, such as floating holidays. This allows team members to choose which holidays they observe based on their personal or cultural preferences. In addition, offering compensatory leave for employees who work on a local holiday ensures fairness across the team.

One regional broadcaster has made it a policy that certain holidays are observed and others throughout the year are not, but the ones missed are made up for with an additional "off work to play" day. These are tied to some of the otherwise long weekends, so that everyone gets a few four-day breaks instead of worrying about observing mid-week holidays.

Navigating global time zones, public holidays, and communication in distributed teams may seem daunting, but with the right strategies and tools, it can be managed smoothly.

Setting Clear Expectations for Availability

One of the biggest hurdles in distributed teams is ensuring team members understand when their colleagues are available. Time zone differences can easily lead to missed opportunities for collaboration or delayed responses if expectations aren't clear.

To overcome this, it's essential to set guidelines for availability and response times. Establishing core hours when team members are expected to be online and responsive can help streamline synchronous communication. For example, a team with members in New York, London, and Sydney might agree on a two-hour window each day when everyone is available. Outside of these hours, asynchronous communication, such as via email or project management tools, can keep work progressing smoothly. The right combination of tools and strategies ensures distributed teams can work efficiently and stay connected, no matter where in the world they are.

CHAPTER 7

Setting up Support Systems for New Members of a Distributed Team

In the world of distributed teams, new hires face a unique set of challenges. Without the traditional office setting, where casual interactions and quick questions can be addressed easily, remote teams may feel isolated or unsure of who to turn to for support. Comprehensive and accessible support systems for new distributed team members are a critical aspect of their integration into the company.

In many instances, a newly hired distributed team member will be used to working remotely or is at least likely to be familiar with the concept. However, they are still new to your company, your way of doing things, your particular meeting rhythms, and also your combined culture based on all those you have in your team.

Let's explore the essential elements of an effective support system for newly hired distributed team members, and how to implement them in a way that ensures a smooth transition and long-term engagement.

Why Support Systems Matter

When your team is spread across different locations, often in various time zones, they can miss out on the informal, everyday interactions that typically help to ease new people into their roles. Distributed team members may struggle to acclimatise to company culture, processes, or even the logistics of their role without a structured support system. Strong onboarding practices and ongoing support systems are essential for keeping distributed teams connected, productive, and aligned with company goals.

Challenges Faced by Newly Hired Members of a Distributed Team

Isolation and disconnection: Without the physical presence of colleagues, new people can feel isolated, which affects morale and performance. The absence of spontaneous interactions – like chats in the break room or quick desk-side questions – can slow their acclimatisation to the team.

Cultural adjustment: Internationally located people often struggle to absorb the nuances of company culture when much of this has developed through a country's culture. Typically, this is what is passed down through daily interactions in a co-located office.

Learning curves with tools and processes: New members of distributed teams may struggle with unfamiliar software or communication platforms, causing delays in their productivity. While it may be that you contracted this new person to have specific skills regarding software, there is still likely potential for learning by either party depending on how each has utilised the software previously. Mixed software programs also provide a particular company culture of use; for example, you might be used to using Zoom and Trello, while your new contractor might be more used to Teams and Dropbox.

Lack of immediate feedback: Distributed teams can miss the instant feedback typical in physical offices, making it harder for them to gauge their performance or know where they need to improve.

To mitigate these challenges, companies must invest in robust support systems. As I've already mentioned, you cannot just place an advert, contract a new person and expect them to simply fit in immediately – regardless of how they came to work with you or where they came from.

Key Elements of an Effective Support System

A dedicated onboarding process: A structured onboarding process is the foundation of a successful support system for new team members. This process should not just introduce the new person to their responsibilities but also ensure they have a clear understanding of the company's culture, communication protocols, and expectations from the start.

Clear onboarding schedule: A well-defined onboarding schedule that includes meetings, introductions, and training sessions should be provided before the new person's first day. (Refer back to Chapter 4.)

Pre-onboarding engagement: Sending a welcome email and providing access to training materials or an onboarding guide before the official start date helps them feel prepared and connected from day one.

Buddy system: Buddies, typically colleagues from different departments, can give personalised guidance that helps new team members navigate the complexities of company processes while fostering cross-departmental relationships.

Regular check-ins: Scheduled check-ins with their buddy allow the new person to ask questions, clarify expectations, and discuss any challenges they face.

Cultural and social integration: The buddy also helps them integrate socially into the company, offering insights into company culture that are difficult to absorb in a remote setting.

Access to HR and IT support: People working remotely need *easy* access to HR and IT support to quickly address issues related to their contract terms, equipment, or software.

HR support: As part of their first day induction, new contractors should be informed about how to contact HR for issues related to contracts, invoicing, benefits and company policies. A designated HR representative for remote contractors ensures that their needs are addressed promptly. If you do not have a dedicated HR person, this contact is most likely you.

Digital contractor handbook: Provide a comprehensive, easily accessible handbook that outlines company policies and procedures. Make sure it is regularly updated to reflect any changes.

Create a central repository or portal: Create a portal where new team members can find all the necessary documentation, guides, training materials, and company policies. This should be easy to navigate and should include FAQs for quick reference.

IT helpdesk: Nothing is more frustrating than having password or access issues to the helpful portals, software and programs and not having a real voice at the end of the line to troubleshoot effectively and efficiently – especially when you're new to the company. A reliable IT support system is essential for distributed team members who may experience technical issues with their hardware, software, or access to company systems. Offering remote IT troubleshooting can ensure that technical problems don't become barriers to productivity.

Self-service resources: Offer a repository of troubleshooting guides, how-to articles, and video tutorials to help your new team members solve common technical issues on their own.

Equipment maintenance and set-up: If your company provides equipment, ensure that there is a system in place to deliver it securely, assist with set-up, and troubleshoot any installation issues.

Mental Health and Well-being Resources

If a new person has recently moved from being an employed salaried person, then it might well be worth having firm mental health and well-being policies in place. Sometimes truly great people jump from a job to a contract and they tick every box you need them to, but if they are simply not quite able to feel part of a solid team, then they may soon want to find another job. Distributed team members who do struggle with work-life balance or feelings of isolation will best be identified through the buddy system, and mental health resources could be vital to their long-term success.

Wellness programs: Virtual wellness programs such as fitness challenges, mindfulness sessions, or mental health workshops can help your distributed team members maintain a healthy work-life balance.

Counselling services: Counselling and mental health support are essential for distributed team members who may feel disconnected from their colleagues and overwhelmed by remote work.

Promote work-life balance: Encourage distributed teams to set boundaries around their work hours and take regular breaks. Establish clear policies that prevent burnout, such as no after-hours emails or mandatory time off after major projects. Again – just because they are self-employed contractors, maybe working at opposing time zones to others in your team – they may struggle to set appropriate boundaries when first starting out, and this may quickly lead to burnout and then reduced productivity. This is also something that your buddy system should be able to help with identifying.

Communication and Collaboration Tools

Clear and effective communication is one of the most important aspects of distributed work. Providing new contractors with the right tools and training them on how to use them ensures smooth collaboration across different locations.

Communication platforms: Tools like Slack, Microsoft Teams, Voxer, and Zoom facilitate real-time communication and help replicate the "water cooler" chats that remote workers miss. They also provide opportunities for group collaboration through video calls, messaging, and shared channels.

Project management tools: Tools like Trello, Asana, or Monday.com help everyone organise their work and track their tasks. Providing training on these tools ensures that new team members can quickly get up to speed on how work is tracked and communicated across teams and projects.

Supporting long-term growth and development

To retain top talent in a distributed team, it's important to provide opportunities for long-term growth and career development. Distributed teams should have access to the same development opportunities as their in-office peers, including training programs, workshops, and mentorship for career progression. You may need to specify in your agreement that you expect self-employed contractors to engage in continued learning and skills updating.

You may also think that offering additional development should be up to each distributed team member. But think of it this way: if you have access to specific industry programs that your distributed team members could benefit from and that in turn could benefit your company, then why hold back? What do you have to gain by *not* offering opportunities for them to advance their skills in your favour?

Some options to consider

Professional development resources: Provide access to online learning platforms like LinkedIn Learning, or company-sponsored workshops and certifications.

Regular performance reviews: Schedule regular check-ins and performance reviews to discuss the distributed team member's progress, offer constructive feedback, and set future career goals.

Internal mobility: Make it clear to distributed team members that there are opportunities for internal advancement. If possible, offer virtual leadership programs or team lead positions to foster their career development within the organisation.

Continuous Feedback and Improvement

Finally, it's important to continuously gather feedback from distributed team members about their experience with the company's support systems. Regular surveys, anonymous feedback channels, and one-on-one conversations can help identify gaps in the support system and opportunities for improvement.

Surveys and feedback tools: Use tools like Google Forms, Scoreapp or SurveyMonkey to collect feedback from new hires on their onboarding experience, the effectiveness of support systems, and their overall satisfaction.

The buddy system: This can easily lead to an ongoing mentorship program, and both can be used to ensure appropriate troubleshooting and feedback is well managed.

Your decision to contract distributed teams should not be thought of as a short-cut option to reduce your overall commitment to being a good manager of the people you have in your company. Just because these remote team members are effectively self-employed contractors, you still have an investment in ensuring they help you achieve more in your company. The more time and effort you put into these onboarding, feedback and support systems, the stronger your company will be, and therefore more productive.

CHAPTER 8

The Buddy System

When onboarding new people into a distributed team, fostering a sense of inclusion and offering support early on can be challenging due to the lack of physical presence. Implementing a buddy system can address this by offering personalised guidance, promoting cross-team collaboration, and integrating new members into the company culture.

One of the best things about using the Buddy System is that it enables you to delegate parts of this process to someone working closely with your new team member, and also develop training skills for you and the buddy to replicate as needed, as your distributed team grows.

How a buddy system enhances the onboarding experience for everyone

By pairing a new team member with a more experienced colleague, companies ensure that new team members have a reliable resource to turn to for guidance on both professional tasks and cultural nuances of your company.

The buddy system provides a structured yet personalised support mechanism to help new team members to:

- **Acclimatise to company culture:** A buddy helps the new person understand how things work, what unwritten rules exist, and how to navigate the company.
- **Feel more engaged and less isolated:** Especially in virtual teams, it can be hard to feel connected. A buddy helps create a sense of community by being someone the new person can turn to for social and professional support. And let's face it, you're likely too busy to be dealing with what is often a quick answer or check in with everyone.
- **Increase their productivity and learn faster:** Having someone readily available to answer questions and share experiences helps new team members become productive faster, minimising downtime caused by confusion or uncertainty.

Buddy Assignment: Careful thought and preparation is required

Selecting the right buddy is crucial for the success of this system. Rather than simply assigning a senior team member, it's often beneficial to assign someone from a different department. This promotes a broader understanding of the company, encourages cross-departmental collaboration, and offers each new person a diverse perspective on how various teams operate.

Key considerations for assigning buddies:

- **Experience level:** Ideally, the buddy should have been with the company for at least a year and be knowledgeable about the company's processes, tools, and culture.
- **Communication skills:** A good buddy should be approachable, patient, and willing to provide feedback. This is not a role that will naturally suit everyone. Some people will excel at it.
- **Workload balance:** Ensure that the buddy has enough time to

dedicate to the new team member. Overburdening a buddy with their regular duties plus this role could dilute the effectiveness of the whole system.

Structuring Buddy/New Team Member Relationships

Regular check-ins allow the new person to discuss any concerns, clarify doubts, or seek advice on specific tasks or processes.

Here's how to structure these check-ins for optimal results:

1. Initial weekly check-ins (first month)

In the first week, you might even make these a *daily* 5- to 10-minute thing. Then following through for the first month, *weekly* check-ins are crucial. These sessions should focus on the immediate needs of the new team members, offering guidance on daily tasks, company processes, and cultural orientation.

These weekly sessions can be limited to 15–20 minutes unless a particular aspect of a project requires more time. However, from the start, reliability around these meetings is important. Otherwise, it is easy for such check-ins to simply fade away too soon, increasing the chance of lack of engagement, avoidable mistakes, and short-term results with your hiring process. All of these can be easily managed, ensuring a robust integration process that pays dividends year after year.

- **Agenda:**
    - **Personal introduction:** Ask how they are feeling, both about the work and adjusting to remote collaboration.
    - **Task clarification:** Ensure the new team member understands their initial tasks and responsibilities.
    - **Company tools and systems:** Offer assistance with software, communication platforms, or tools that are critical for the role.
    - **Social integration:** Discuss the company culture, unwrit-

ten rules, and how team members typically communicate and collaborate remotely.

- **Encourage questions:** Create a safe space for the new person to ask questions, even ones they may feel are trivial.

- **Next steps:** Set goals for the coming week, making sure the new member feels prepared.

2. Bi-weekly check-ins (second and third months)

Once the new team member has settled into their role, bi-weekly check-ins can focus on deeper integration, ongoing support, and feedback.

- **Agenda:**

  - **Progress review:** Check how the new person is progressing with their tasks and goals. Offer feedback or help on any challenges.

  - **Cross-department insights:** Encourage the new member to reach out to other teams or join cross-functional meetings, expanding their understanding of the business as a whole.

  - **Cultural deep dive:** Discuss more about the company's history, mission, and values, and how they are lived out day to day.

  - **Long-term goals:** Start discussing career development or personal goals within the company.

  - **Feedback solicitation:** Ask how the buddy system is working for them and whether they need additional resources or support.

3. Monthly check-ins (after the first quarter)

At this stage, the new person should be more confident, and check-ins can be scaled back to monthly sessions. These should focus on ongoing professional development and fine-tuning their integration into the broader team.

- **Agenda:**

  - **Reflection on past progress:** Review the last month's work, challenges, and successes.

  - **Professional development:** Discuss opportunities for growth, such as training programs, mentorship, or taking on more responsibility.

  - **Company involvement:** Encourage participation in team-building activities, company-wide events, or special projects.

  - **Feedback:** Continue to ask for feedback on their experience with the buddy system, and adjust the approach if necessary.

4. Open communication between check-ins

Encourage every team member to reach out anytime between scheduled meetings. This ensures that they feel supported and can get help promptly if issues arise.

Key Tips for Successful Check-ins

- **Prepare an agenda:** Both the buddy and the new person should come prepared to discuss key points.
- **Set clear outcomes:** After each session, agree on specific tasks, areas of improvement, or next steps.
- **Keep it structured but informal:** The buddy system is meant to offer guidance, so keep it relaxed but ensure the new member is benefiting from the support.

While it might seem a lot like overkill, having a written agenda for the buddy to work through for every meeting ensures the questions that need to be addressed and the support that needs to be given happens. As time goes on, it's more likely that without a written agenda, the conversation might just meander meaninglessly.

Feedback loops: To improve the buddy system continually, gather feedback from both buddies and new members. This can be done through short surveys or direct conversations. The insights will help refine the program, ensuring it meets the needs of both the new team member and the buddies.

You also have the need for feedback from the buddy assigned to look out for the new person. Having a written agenda ensures that you get that feedback in ways that really matter and can be managed by you if necessary.

In distributed teams, the buddy system is an invaluable tool for ensuring new team members feel welcomed, supported, and engaged.

By carefully selecting buddies, structuring regular check-ins, and maintaining an open feedback loop, you can create an environment where new team members are set up for long-term success. Through a buddy's support, new team members can integrate more seamlessly into both the professional and social fabric of the company, ultimately driving higher retention and productivity in your distributed workforce.

Buddy Check-in Agenda Checklist

Weekly check-ins (first month) questions the buddy can ask to ensure that all necessary information is captured.

1. **Welcome and well-being**
   - How are you feeling about your role so far?
   - Any challenges adjusting to the remote work set-up or company processes?

2. **Task and role clarification**
   - Are there any tasks you're unclear about or need more guidance on?
   - Do you have any questions about tools or systems you're using?

3. **Company tools and processes**
   - Do you need additional help with communication tools (Slack, email, project management platforms)?
   - Are you comfortable using the tools and software?

4. **Cultural insights**
   - Discuss any unwritten rules or nuances of the company culture.
   - Are there any concerns about team dynamics or communication styles?

5. **Questions and feedback**
   - Do you have any questions about your role or the company?
   - How can I assist you further?
6. **Next steps**
   - Set small goals for the upcoming week.
   - Plan tasks or areas to focus on before the next check-in.

NOTES:

Monthly check-ins (after first three months)

Focus on continuous growth, professional development, and feedback.

1. **Reflection on progress**
   - How do you feel about your progress over the last month?
   - What were your major accomplishments? Any challenges or areas for improvement?
2. **Professional development**
   - Are there any training or development opportunities you're interested in pursuing?
   - Do you need help accessing learning resources or connecting with a mentor?
3. **Company engagement**
   - Have you been able to participate in company-wide or team events (virtual meetups, team-building activities)?
   - Are there any areas of the company you'd like to explore further or get involved in?
4. **Long-term goals**
   - How are you feeling about your long-term career goals within this company?

- Do you need support in setting or achieving any new personal or professional goals?

5. **Feedback and continuous improvement**

   - How can the buddy system or onboarding process be improved for future hires?
   - Do you feel fully integrated into the team? If not, what can we do to help?

6. **Next steps**

   - Set monthly objectives.
   - Identify opportunities to take on new projects or leadership roles.

This checklist helps structure each meeting and ensures that key aspects of onboarding, cultural integration and role development are covered. Buddies can customise the list depending on the new hire's needs but should aim to follow the general structure to ensure consistency.

Depending on the role of the new distributed team member, you may not need all these questions, but tailor a similar agenda to suit your needs, and discuss this with your buddy so they understand what is needed from them to ensure that this system works well for your company.

CHAPTER 9

Team-Building Tools and Opportunities

In-house location-based employees need to be united as a team, but so do remote and distributed team members. Teams don't happen by accident, and the more effort you put into developing and nurturing great teamwork, the better your results will be for your company overall.

So, let's explore some practical tools and activities that can enhance team dynamics, boost morale, and create a stronger sense of community among distributed teams.

Quizzes and Polls

Using quizzes to reinforce key concepts after training sessions can significantly improve knowledge retention. Tools like **Google Forms**, **Kahoot**, Scoreapp or **Quizlet** allow you to create engaging, interactive quizzes that not only test knowledge but make the process fun. When team members are quizzed on important material, they become more invested in understanding the content fully, ensuring that learning sticks. Providing immediate feedback on quiz answers helps team members quickly understand their mistakes and learn the correct information.

Teaming up pairs or small groups to work together on quizzes is a powerful team-building exercise. You can run an ongoing monthly leaderboard for quizzes too, introducing a friendly rivalry within divisions of your company.

Quizzes and polls serve as powerful tools to reinforce key concepts and ensure that team members retain important information after training sessions. By integrating these tools into your remote team training strategy, you can transform passive learning into an interactive experience, which fosters better engagement and knowledge retention.

Polls can also be used during live training sessions or virtual meetings to gauge understanding and maintain engagement. They help ensure everyone is on the same page and encourage participation, even from quieter members. Platforms such as **Zoom** or **Microsoft Teams** have built-in poll features that make it easy to run quick, interactive surveys to keep the team involved and active in the session.

Five great reasons to use quizzes and polls

1. **Active engagement:** Quizzes require participants to actively recall information, strengthening their memory and understanding of key concepts.

2. **Immediate feedback:** Offering instant feedback allows team members to quickly identify mistakes, correct their understanding and reinforce correct knowledge.

3. **Boost accountability:** When team members know that they will be quizzed on important topics, they pay closer attention during training sessions.

4. **Increased retention**: Studies show that active recall, such as answering quiz questions, can significantly improve long-term retention of information.

Tracking progress: Quizzes give you a measurable way to track your team's progress, ensuring that everyone is aligned on key topics before moving on to more advanced content.

Learn more about building your own Quiz on page 84.

Virtual Scavenger Hunts

Interactive exploration

A virtual scavenger hunt is an excellent way to encourage your team to explore different areas of your company's resources, such as the intranet, company website, or internal documentation. This not only helps familiarise them with tools but also makes learning more dynamic and engaging.

You can also run a Virtual Scavenger Hunt as part of a quiz. For example, direct teams or individuals to locate a particular set of instructions or code in your website, to build a complete picture of something. Or invite them to find a particular piece of company, industry, or geographical history to base a three-minute presentation on.

Team collaboration

Design tasks that require collaboration to complete. For example, create clues or questions that team members must answer together, encouraging them to interact with one another. This can help break down silos, build rapport, and foster teamwork, especially in teams that are geographically dispersed.

Rewards for participation

To encourage participation, consider offering small incentives or recognition for teams or individuals who complete the scavenger hunt successfully. Rewards such as virtual badges, gift cards, or public recognition during meetings can motivate and excite your team members.

Gamification

Progress tracking with gamified elements

Gamification adds an element of fun and motivation to learning and daily tasks. Implementing tools like **badges**, **leaderboards**, or **points systems** can track progress and encourage friendly competition. This is particularly effective for tasks or learning modules where long-term engagement is needed.

Recognition of achievements

Celebrating accomplishments with **digital badges** or **certificates** can help reinforce a sense of achievement and pride. Tools like **BadgeOS** or **Credly** allow you to manage and award these recognitions, adding value to everyday tasks or training completions.

Interactive Learning Platforms

Platforms like **Duolingo** for language skills or **Codecademy** for coding can offer a gamified approach to learning that keeps team members engaged and progressing at their own pace. Consider asking your internationally located team members to learn basic greetings in each other's languages as a starting point. Using Duolingo for this can result in a very friendly competitiveness within groups all learning languages at the same time – what a useful skillset to foster!

Why not assign an annual task-team to create a simple but enjoyable quiz, virtual scavenger hunt and gamification option that combines what everyone wants to learn with how they want to work the idea. That way the distributed team members have to work together to create a workable plan that everyone buys into.

Breakout Rooms and Group Discussions

Small group interaction

Breakout rooms during virtual meetings can encourage deeper discussion in smaller groups. By splitting the team into smaller, more manageable groups, everyone has an opportunity to contribute more meaningfully. These sessions help build closer connections between team members and foster active participation. Zoom makes it easy to do this within their meetings, and some brief planning before each meeting helps to ensure that the flow is well managed.

Ensure that breakout room sessions have clear instructions and objectives. Structured activities such as problem-solving exercises, brainstorming sessions, or scenario-based discussions can make these interactions more productive. Assigning facilitators to each room can further ensure that discussions remain focused and relevant.

After each breakout activity, hold debrief sessions where each group shares their insights with the larger team. This practice not only reinforces learning but also brings different perspectives into the conversation, enriching the experience for everyone.

Interactive Whiteboards

Collaborative tools

Interactive whiteboards, such as **Miro**, **MURAL**, or **Microsoft Whiteboard**, provide an excellent space for brainstorming, collaborative projects, and visual presentations. These tools allow team members to work together in real time, regardless of their physical location, making brainstorming sessions more dynamic and visually engaging.

Interactive whiteboards allow multiple users to contribute ideas, give feedback, and refine concepts in real time, creating a more engaging and collaborative environment. This helps foster creativity and collective problem-solving among team members. Using visual aids like diagrams, flowcharts, and mind maps on interactive whiteboards enhances understanding and retention of complex topics. This visual approach is especially helpful in technical discussions or strategic planning sessions.

Role-Playing Exercises

Simulate real scenarios

Role-playing exercises that simulate real workplace scenarios can provide team members with valuable practice and help them develop new skills in a safe environment. Whether it's handling customer service enquiries, managing project deadlines, or navigating difficult conversations, role-playing allows people to gain hands-on experience without risk. When you have to step into another department or another person's shoes, you get a greater understanding of what their particular issues are. For example, if the sales team had to role play the problem-solving skills of the customer service team, they might discover the value of gathering information and filling in *all* the details on forms when completing a sale.

Feedback and reflection

After each exercise, provide detailed feedback on performance and encourage self-reflection. This gives team members the opportunity to identify areas for improvement while building confidence in their abilities.

Making it enjoyable

By introducing different roles and challenges, you can keep these exercises enjoyable and engaging. Incorporating humour or gamification elements can make learning and development not only effective but fun. It might seem like a lot of work to invest in developing great teams, but eventually, this will pay off in many ways. Increased learning, performance, collaboration and innovation are just the start. Distributed teams who love their work, and working with your company, will not only stay longer, but they also often know just who else is worth putting forward to join the team as you grow.

Effective team building for distributed teams involves leveraging a variety of interactive tools and activities to engage team members, promote collaboration, and reinforce learning. From quizzes to virtual scavenger hunts, gamified learning platforms, and role-playing exercises, the right combination of activities can enhance remote team dynamics and create a more cohesive, motivated, and high-performing group.

How to Create Effective Team-Building Quizzes

To create effective quizzes that reinforce learning, consider the following steps:

1. **Identify key concepts**: Focus on the most important takeaways from your training sessions. These are the concepts that you want team members to fully understand and retain.

2. **Mix question types:** Use a variety of question formats to keep the quiz engaging and test different levels of understanding. Include multiple-choice, true/false, fill-in-the-blank, and short answer questions.

3. **Use engaging platforms:** Platforms like **Google Forms**, **Kahoot**, and **Quizlet** allow you to create visually appealing quizzes that are easy to distribute and complete.

4. **Offer immediate feedback:** For each question, provide immediate feedback explaining why a particular answer is right or wrong.

5. **Gamify the experience:** Adding elements of gamification, like leaderboards or point systems, can motivate team members to perform better and stay engaged.

Example: Creating an engaging quiz

Let's assume you've just completed a training session on "Effective Communication in Distributed Teams". Here's how you could create a quiz to reinforce key concepts from the session:

Example Quiz: Effective Communication in Distributed Teams

Instructions:

Please answer the following questions to test your understanding of the key concepts discussed during the training session. You will receive immediate feedback on your answers.

1. **What is the most effective way to ensure clear communication in a distributed team?**
   - a) Use only emails to communicate
   - b) Schedule regular video meetings and use project management tools
   - c) Avoid real-time communication and focus only on asynchronous methods
   - d) Delegate all communication to the team lead

Correct answer: b) Schedule regular video meetings and use project management tools

Feedback: Regular video meetings combined with project management tools ensure that all team members are aligned and that tasks are clearly communicated.

2. **True or false? Asynchronous communication is ideal for quick, urgent updates in remote teams.**
   - a) True
   - b) False

Correct answer: False

Feedback: Asynchronous communication is typically better for non-urgent updates. For quick, urgent updates, real-time communication like messaging or video calls are more effective.

3. **Fill in the blank: In a distributed team, it's important to set clear _____ to avoid misunderstandings and ensure accountability.**

Correct answer: Expectations

Feedback: Setting clear expectations regarding tasks, deadlines and responsibilities is key to avoiding misunderstandings in a distributed team.

4. **Which of the following is NOT a best practice for communication in distributed teams?**
   - a) Using a single channel for all communication
   - b) Having regular check-ins with the team
   - c) Encouraging open feedback and questions
   - d) Clarifying goals and deadlines upfront

Correct answer: a) Using a single channel for all communication
Feedback: Relying on only one communication channel can lead to bottlenecks and missed messages. It's better to use a combination of tools like email, messaging apps, and video calls depending on the context.

5. **Poll Question:** On a scale of 1–5, (where 1 is "not confident at all" and 5 is ""very confident"), **how confident do you feel about using asynchronous communication tools effectively?**

After polling, the results will guide further training or support in this area.

Post-Quiz Feedback:

Congratulations on completing the quiz! If you scored 80% or higher, you're well on your way to mastering effective communication in distributed teams. If you scored below 80%, don't worry – review the feedback provided and feel free to revisit the training materials. Let's keep building those communication skills!

Customizing the quiz experience

To enhance the effectiveness of your quizzes:

- **Set a time limit**: For more advanced quizzes, adding a time limit can challenge team members and prompt them to think quickly and effectively.
- **Randomise questions**: Shuffle the order of questions or answers to prevent patterns and encourage focus.
- **Leaderboards**: For competitive teams, consider introducing a leaderboard that ranks participants based on their quiz scores, adding a healthy element of competition.

By incorporating well-structured quizzes and offering immediate feedback, you create an engaging learning environment that encourages active participation and helps team members retain important knowledge. Quizzes are not only an assessment tool but also a reinforcement mechanism that motivates distributed team members to stay engaged in their learning and growth together.

CHAPTER 10

The Importance of Cybersecurity

The shift to working with remotely located team members has brought numerous benefits, from increased flexibility to a more global work-force. However, it has also introduced significant cybersecurity challenges. In traditional office environments, companies can closely monitor and control security protocols, but with distributed teams, individual team members work from various locations, using a mix of personal and company-provided devices. This decentralisation opens up a range of vulnerabilities that can be exploited by cybercriminals.

One critical issue in remote work is the increased risk of *phishing attacks*. Without the immediate oversight of IT departments, remote people are more vulnerable to sophisticated phishing schemes designed to steal sensitive information, such as login credentials or financial data. Cybercriminals have also been quick to capitalise on remote work trends, using work-related topics to create convincing fake emails that trick people into clicking malicious links.

It's become a very sophisticated, dark industry that threatens many unaware companies.

Another significant challenge is unsecured networks. Distributed team members often connect from public Wi-Fi networks or home set-ups that lack the stringent security protocols found in office environments. This can expose company data to interception, especially when people are accessing sensitive systems without the use of a secure Virtual Private Network (VPN). Even home Wi-Fi networks, while more secure than public hotspots, can be compromised if proper security settings are not in place.

Remote work also increases the potential for device vulnerabilities. Many people use personal devices that might not have the same level of security as corporate-issued hardware. These devices may lack proper encryption, security patches, or the latest software updates, making them prime targets for malware or ransomware attacks.

The growing complexity of cybersecurity threats makes it crucial for companies to implement strong security protocols for their remote teams. Training your people to recognise potential risks, enforcing the use of encrypted communication channels, and providing secure tools for collaboration and data sharing are essential strategies for mitigating these risks. As remotely based work continues to evolve, robust cybersecurity for every team member, regardless of location, is no longer optional – it's non-negotiable.

Let's explore the key risks and some very practical solutions for maintaining cybersecurity across distributed teams, empowering individual members to protect both their own personal data and your company data.

Securing Remote Work Environments

In the context of remotely located team members on an international scale and local to any country, the rules of "can't be too careful" apply. Securing the digital workspace for individual team members is essential to maintaining the overall cybersecurity for your company.

One of the most critical steps is enforcing multi-factor authentication (MFA). MFA adds an extra layer of security beyond just passwords, ensuring that even if a hacker gains access to login credentials, they still require an additional form of authentication, such as a mobile app code or biometric scan. This dramatically reduces the risk of unauthorised access to company systems.

MFA: I recommend talking with a cyber security specialist to decide on the easiest way to do this, so that your team is supported and secure without any of your team members also being able to mess it up. For example, if someone is let go from a contract early or they suffer an accident rendering them unable to work for any period of time, you don't want to risk not being able to retain some control over their network or your content.

Password management: All members of your team should use strong, unique passwords for different services, and password managers should be introduced to store and generate complex passwords securely. Using common or repeated passwords across accounts leaves everyone highly vulnerable to credential-stuffing attacks, where compromised credentials from one site are used to access another.

Device encryption: This is crucial, particularly for remote workers who use laptops, phones, or tablets to access sensitive company data. Should a device be lost or stolen, encryption ensures that any data stored on the device remains inaccessible to unauthorised users. Most modern devices come with built-in encryption tools, but organisations must ensure that all remote employees have this feature enabled and understand how to use it properly.

This is also where a conversation with and securing the services of a cyber security specialist can be very helpful.

Virtual Private Networks (VPNs): Whenever your contractors access company systems from unsecured locations, such as public Wi-Fi or home networks, it is essential they use a VPN. A VPN encrypts internet traffic, creating a secure tunnel for data to pass through, which prevents cybercriminals from intercepting sensitive information. VPNs are particularly important for protecting proprietary data, login credentials, and confidential communications.

Larger organisations may also consider setting up remote servers for each team member to access sensitive client or company data, tools or subscriptions.

Regular software updates: Ensuring that all devices have the latest security patches reduces the risk of exploitation through known vulnerabilities. Many successful cyberattacks occur because people delay or ignore updates. Educating team members on the importance of immediate updates to operating systems, browsers, and apps is an important step in minimising risks in a remote work environment.

One small note of caution: Automated updates can be problematic with your team members firing up their device at the start of their day, only to lose a significant amount of time while a large update takes place on their device. We learned this lesson the hard way in the early days at Prominence. We now have a protocol where automatic updates are to be deactivated, and a manual update instigated by each team member every Friday afternoon at the end of their day.

Secure Communication Channels

With the rise of collaboration platforms, email, and video conferencing tools, distributed team members often exchange sensitive information across various platforms, making them a prime target for cyberattacks. Ensuring that these communications are encrypted and secure is crucial to maintaining confidentiality and protecting company data.

First, you should mandate the use of encrypted messaging tools.

Standard email platforms are not always secure by default, making sensitive information susceptible to interception. Companies should opt for platforms that offer end-to-end encryption, meaning only the sender and the recipient can read the messages. This is particularly important for communications involving financial data, trade secrets, or personal information.

Training team members *and all your employees at all levels* in your organisation to recognise phishing emails and fraudulent messages is vital. Cybercriminals often impersonate colleagues or company officials to trick employees into sharing sensitive information or clicking on malicious links. Remote team members should be taught to scrutinise the sender's email address, avoid downloading unsolicited attachments, and never provide sensitive data unless they can verify the source. Your company can support this by running regular phishing simulations to test and reinforce awareness. As also outlined in the chapters about developing a strong culture through gaming to build better virtual connections and collaboration, incorporating the training around cybersecurity can only help your company. There is no downside to taking this seriously!

Secure video conferencing tools are another necessary component for remote team communication. With the surge in video calls, particularly during the COVID-19 pandemic, platforms such as Zoom and Microsoft Teams became integral to remote work. However, not all video conferencing platforms provide adequate security features. It is important to ensure these tools offer end-to-end encryption and password protection for meetings, which prevents unauthorised access or eavesdropping on private company discussions.

Lastly, organisations should develop data-sharing protocols that emphasise the use of encrypted file-sharing services like Dropbox Business or Google Workspace, which have robust security settings. Employees should be encouraged to avoid sharing sensitive files over unsecured channels like personal email or non-corporate messaging apps.

If you are going to use any of these platforms, ensure you have someone in your team who is an expert at setting up the accounts and knows how to utilise the built-in security features of all these options. If no one on your team is able to do that, train someone or consult an outside expert.

A case study you do not want to replicate:

An organisation that became a client of Prominence had (prior to becoming a client) a disgruntled team member who was still part of their local team. This team member was maliciously accessing social media accounts after hours.

The content and activity that was occurring on the accounts was unprofessional, to say the least. The team member would then change the password access to the accounts to prevent easy removal of the malicious content and comments.

It took a number of weeks to discover who the culprit was and remove them from the business and social media accounts before significant brand damage occurred. They have now replaced the team member and implemented procedures that mitigate these risks. One key protocol was to activate MFA for all social media accounts that required a code sent to a dedicated mobile device that only the founder or trusted family members could access.

Who should have admin access to your online accounts?

Most subscriptions and social media platforms offer different levels of access. It is wise to avoid giving top-level access to anyone who does not need it.

Let's use LinkedIn as an example.

On LinkedIn, there are several administrative roles for managing a LinkedIn Page, each with specific permissions. Here are the different admin levels available:

1. Super admin
- Full control over the page.
- Can edit the page, add or remove admins, and access all analytics.
- Has the ability to manage all page settings, including updating company information and changing the page's logo.

2. Content admin
- Can create and manage content for the page (posts, articles, updates).
- Has permission to engage with followers through comments, reactions, and messages.
- Has access to view the page's analytics.

3. Analyst
- Can only view analytics related to the LinkedIn page, but cannot post or manage content.
- Ideal for someone who needs insight into performance without the ability to make changes to the page.

4. Curator (Talent admin)
- Specific to LinkedIn Career Pages. This admin can edit career sections of the page (such as job posts) and access relevant analytics.
- Focuses on the talent acquisition aspect of the LinkedIn Page.

5. Recruiter admin (Job admin)

- Can manage job postings on the page.
- Has permission to view and respond to applications, edit job postings, and access the company's job analytics.

These roles help teams with multiple people manage a LinkedIn company page effectively. Each role's permissions are defined by LinkedIn to ensure clear separation of responsibilities.

Ensure you are aware of all options for admin access and only provide the level each team member requires. Having this protocol in place makes your team aware that you are taking security seriously, which lessens the chance of malicious activity.

Incident Response Plans for Remote Teams

Cybersecurity threats like phishing, malware, or ransomware can affect team members working from various locations, and a well-structured plan ensures that incidents are addressed swiftly and systematically. Since remote team members may not have immediate access to IT staff, they must be empowered with a simple and accessible response protocol.

The first step in an incident response plan is awareness. Team members should be trained to recognise the signs of a potential breach, such as unusual system behaviour, unexpected requests for sensitive information, or abnormal login attempts. Everyone should recognise the importance of immediate reporting, ensuring that suspicious activity is communicated without delay to the IT team or, in the case of smaller organisations, the founder.

The IT department must be equipped to respond to incidents remotely, using tools to assess the scope of the breach, contain the threat, and mitigate any potential damage. Following the incident, companies should conduct a post-incident review to identify vulnerabilities and strengthen security protocols.

Checklist for an Incident Response Plan:

1. Immediate reporting process: Ensure you have clearly written and understood instructions for anyone on your team to report incidents.

2. Contact list: Have a designated point of contact within the IT or security team.

3. Containment steps: Plan what quick actions will limit the spread of the threat.

4. Remote access for IT: Create effective tools and protocols for the IT team to manage incidents from afar.

5. Post-incident review: Ensure you have a solid review process to update security protocols and prevent future issues.

CHAPTER 11

How to Find Candidates for your Distributed Team

Finding talented team members across borders presents a unique opportunity to tap into diverse skill sets, cultures, and working styles. I have outlined many roles that you may consider finding the right candidates for, yet it requires a thoughtful approach. This chapter will guide you through the various ways to source talented individuals for your distributed team.

If your need is for a one-off project or very short project-style engagements, services like Upwork, Freelancer, or 99 Designs may be your best option. They have a good process for candidate selection and security features to ensure your tasks are completed to your satisfaction before payments are released to your contractor.

However, you will find the process for ongoing communication and longer-term engagement cumbersome and expensive. It may present a good opportunity to test the waters on working with remote team members to get a feel for the process and outcomes you can expect.

Once you have decided to go beyond short-term project contracts, it's time to find your new candidates. Here are some options you might consider if you prefer the DIY option.

1. Online job portals

Online job portals allow you to post job openings, search for specific skills, and engage directly with potential people in specific regions.

- **Philippines:** The Philippines has several job boards and freelance platforms such as OnlineJobs.ph and JobStreet.
- **India:** India: Websites like Naukri and Indeed India are good options.
- **Eastern Europe:** Platforms such as WeWorkRemotely and RemoteOK are ideal for sourcing tech talent. For more country-specific searches, consider using sites like NoFluffJobs in Poland or Pracuj.pl for roles in Romania.
- **South Africa:** Platforms like Careers24, PNet, and Indeed South Africa provide access to qualified candidates across industries.
- Remote.co and AngelList are also excellent resources.

2. LinkedIn Talent Solutions

LinkedIn has grown into one of the most powerful tools for recruitment worldwide. By using LinkedIn Talent Solutions, you can narrow your search based on location, industry, skills, and experience.

LinkedIn also provides the option to post job listings across the platform, giving your opportunity greater visibility in the global market.

3. Local networking and communities

Networking remains a powerful tool in recruitment. Local meetups and professional communities can provide direct access to potential candidates, as well as insight into the regional job market.

- **Tech meetups:** In regions like India and Eastern Europe, tech meetups and conferences offer direct access to developers, engineers, and other tech professionals. Websites such as Meetup and Eventbrite list these events, which are often a goldmine for finding qualified talent.

- **University and alumni networks:** Partnering with universities can be a strategic move, especially if you are seeking younger talent with fresh ideas. Many universities maintain strong alumni networks that can help you identify top graduates in regions like South Africa and Eastern Europe.

4. Social media and professional networks

In some countries, social media platforms are highly integrated into the job search process.

- **India and the Philippines:** Facebook is widely used for job hunting in both India and the Philippines. Many professionals in these regions join specific groups focused on freelance work, virtual assistance, or industry-specific opportunities. It's worth exploring these groups for direct engagement with potential candidates.

- **Eastern Europe:** Tech talent in Eastern Europe often congregates on platforms like GitHub and Stack Overflow. These sites not only serve as recruitment tools but also as a way to assess candidates' portfolios and contributions to open-source projects.

5. Team referrals

Once you have a few distributed team members, one of the most effective ways to source high-quality candidates is through word of mouth. Encouraging your current team, particularly those from the regions you're targeting, to refer candidates from their networks can lead to excellent hires. Referred candidates often come pre-vetted by your team, saving you time during the recruitment process.

Potential Hazards of Using Online Platforms and Hiring Directly

While online job portals and freelance platforms provide access to a global pool of talent, sourcing directly through these platforms comes with certain risks. Understanding these potential hazards is crucial for mitigating challenges and ensuring a successful search.

1. Communication and cultural barriers

Building distributed teams globally means working across different languages, time zones, and cultural contexts. Misunderstandings may arise due to differences in communication styles, cultural expectations, or even language proficiency. In countries like India and the Philippines, English is widely spoken, but subtle cultural differences in communication can still lead to confusion, especially when it comes to expectations around working hours, deadlines, and feedback.

Solution: It is important to evaluate a candidate's communication skills in the context of your business needs. Conduct video interviews to assess fluency and comfort with English (or the language of your business). Establish clear communication channels and cultural sensitivity training to ensure smoother collaboration.

2. Time zone and availability challenges

Time zone differences can impact real-time communication. A candidate from the Philippines will be on the opposite side of the globe from a company based in Europe, making it challenging to coordinate meetings or deal with urgent matters.

Solution: Clearly articulate the country your business is located in and the time zone difference between you and the potential candidate's country. Outline why communication may be slower than usual, so they have clear expectations on response times.

3. Managing currency differences

Navigating the differences in currency values can present both challenges and opportunities. Exchange rates fluctuate, and the cost of living in many countries will vary widely. To ensure fair and competitive compensation while managing the impact of currency differences on your business, it's important to consider the following:

Local market rates

Income expectations can differ significantly across regions, depending on the local cost of living, demand for skills, and industry norms. Before hiring in different countries, research local salary standards for the role you're hiring for. Websites such as **Glassdoor**, **PayScale**, or regional job boards can help you gather insights into standard compensation ranges in these areas.

By aligning your offer with local market rates, you ensure that the position is attractive to candidates while also maintaining cost efficiency. Keep in mind that competitive pay in one country might be perceived as either low or high in another.

Advertised remuneration

One of the biggest mistakes I see is advertising for roles in the currency of the business looking for team members. Often your team members will have no concept of what they might be worth in your local currency. You risk them not applying as your advertised remuneration seems too low, or else going through the vetting process in-depth, only to withdraw due to unrealistic expectations once they fully understand your offer.

I suggest you do the exchange rate conversion and promote your offer in their local currency. Make it very clear whether you're offering monthly or annual remuneration. Quite likely you will not plan to make the monthly payments in their local currency, and you can be more explicit about this once you get into one-to-one interactions about the role.

Hiring internationally is no longer a challenge limited to large corporations. With the right resources and strategies, businesses of any size can find talented professionals in many countries. By leveraging online platforms, local expertise, and global networks, you can build a diverse and capable team that supports your business objectives across borders.

A Done-For-You Option

I have outlined how you can go about finding talented team members yourself and some of the pitfalls to be mindful of. If that seems too time consuming or getting it wrong is a strong possibility, we can help. Prominence Global has a service called Remote Team Connect that can take care of the process for you.

The first step is to ascertain whether you and your business are ready to consider adding distributed team members. To this end, we have created a simple assessment you can use.

So, type this URL into your device now and take the 2-minute assessment, then come back to this chapter.

https://assessment.prominence.global/distributed-teams

If you scored a passing grade, here's the next step:

Unlock the potential of building your Distributed Team with Prominence Global details are at the end of Chapter 12 .

There are three important points to make here:

- **We bridge the distance between Western businesses and top-tier talent globally.** Experience seamless integration of highly skilled professionals into your workforce, all working remotely to drive your business forward.

- **We harness the power of LinkedIn, the world's largest professional network, to source candidates who match your specific needs – quickly.** Our unique approach ensures that we not only reach a vast audience but also target the most qualified professionals.

- **We are not a recruitment agency; we are your marketing partner.**

CHAPTER 12

Setting Clear Expectations

A Guide for Team Members and Managers

As distributed teams become more prevalent, setting clear expectations between team members and managers is crucial for ensuring smooth operations, maintaining productivity, and fostering a positive work environment. Both sides must understand their roles, responsibilities, and the value of distributed work. This clarity helps avoid misunderstandings, manage workloads effectively, and leverage the benefits of working across geographies.

Expectations for Distributed Team Members

1. Flexibility and self-management

For distributed team members, flexibility is both a benefit and a responsibility. Working from different locations often comes with the freedom to create a more balanced work-life schedule, but this also requires a strong sense of self-management. Team members are expected to organise their time, prioritise tasks effectively, and meet deadlines without direct supervision. Managers rely on contractors to maintain productivity independently, so personal accountability and time management skills are essential.

2. Clear and transparent communication

Remote team members are also expected to be proactive in communication. Since managers and associated members aren't physically present, it's up to the contractor to regularly update their progress, ask questions, and clarify any ambiguities in their tasks. Tools like **Slack**, **Asana**, or **Trello** provide platforms for team members to stay engaged and connected. Clear communication, especially in asynchronous work environments, ensures that projects move forward smoothly, even when direct, real-time interaction is not possible.

Furthermore, distributed team members must be transparent about their availability. Since all people in the team may work in various time zones, it's crucial that everyone knows when they are available for meetings or to respond to queries. Setting a clear availability status on messaging platforms or sharing personal working hours helps ensure that communication is streamlined and efficient.

3. Accountability and delivery of results

Without the immediate oversight of an office environment, distributed team members are often judged more on results than on the process. Therefore, a strong focus on delivering quality work on time is essential. Distributed team members are expected to hit their deadlines, complete tasks as assigned, and take ownership of their responsibilities as per their contracted agreement. Whether the task requires collaboration with others or independent work, team members must demonstrate a high level of professionalism and commitment to the outcomes expected of them.

Expectations for Managers of Distributed Teams

1. Providing flexibility and support

While distributed team members are responsible for managing their work schedules, managers are expected to provide the flexibility needed to accommodate different time zones and working conditions. This flexibility should extend to scheduling meetings, deadlines, and workload expectations. Managers should recognise that distributed team members may not always be available during typical office hours, and they must be open to asynchronous work styles. By offering flexible deadlines and encouraging work-life balance, managers can create an environment where all members of the distributed team can feel valued.

2. Establishing clear goals and communication standards

Managers play a key role in setting the tone for communication within distributed teams. They must clearly outline the expectations for how often team members should check in, report progress, and raise concerns. A transparent communication strategy should include how frequently team meetings will take place, the primary communication channels (such as Slack or Microsoft Teams), and the expected response times for emails or messages.

Managers should also ensure that goals are clearly defined and measurable. Setting SMART goals (Specific, Measurable, Achievable, Relevant, Time-bound) helps remotely located members understand exactly what is expected of them and how their performance will be evaluated. This clarity is especially important when team members work across different time zones and may not have immediate access to their managers for feedback or guidance.

Just assuming that you are paying an independent contractor to complete a project or be part of your team means you don't have to consider their overall involvement in the big picture of what you're aiming to achieve with your distributed team. If they do a great job, then you might want to involve them with longer term or bigger opportunities in the future. You may be having them as contractors for only one or a long-term project and things can change, but it is your responsibility to manage this relationship, just as it is their responsibility to do so in return.

Finding and attracting great people is only part of the process. Keeping the great ones is a core part of your objective too.

3. Building trust and fostering collaboration

Trust is a critical element in managing distributed teams. Managers need to trust their team members to manage their time, meet deadlines, and communicate effectively without micromanagement. Fostering this trust begins by providing team members with the autonomy to make decisions within their scope of work. This empowerment encourages initiative and responsibility, which are essential qualities for successful remote work.

In addition to building trust, managers must also work to foster collaboration among distributed team members. Virtual team-building activities, regular check-ins, and encouraging informal interactions (such as virtual coffee chats) can help build a strong sense of connection within the team. Collaboration tools such as Trello, Zoom, and Slack also make it easier to maintain transparency and ensure that all team members have the same access to information, no matter where they are located.

4. Providing feedback and recognition

Feedback is a cornerstone of all team development, and it's just as important in distributed teams as it is in traditional office environments. Managers must ensure that remote people receive regular feedback on their input into the projects and work undertaken too. Constructive feedback helps team members understand how they can improve and grow as part of your ongoing needs for their services, while positive recognition for a job well done can boost morale and engagement.

Distributed team members, just like employees do, want to feel recognised for their contributions. Since remote workers often miss out on the casual praise or feedback that can occur in an office setting, managers need to make a deliberate effort to acknowledge achievements and successes. Whether through public praise in team meetings, a simple message of thanks, or a formal recognition program, celebrating accomplishments is key to maintaining motivation in a distributed work environment.

One company I know has clients who are award-winning, and there is a process to enter those awards that relies on the input of the contracted copywriter and a designer. They also do grant applications. When their clients are successful with contracts, awards, or grants, everyone celebrates, and the clients are also aware of the input by the entire team. This is great for the individual contractors to have on their own resumes and marketing materials for their other pursuits of contracts as distributed team members.

The Value of Distributed Teams

Both managers and team members stand to benefit greatly from the distributed team model when expectations are clearly defined and managed effectively. For team members, distributed work offers the flexibility to balance personal and professional responsibilities, while also providing access to global job opportunities. For managers and organisations, distributed teams provide access to a broader talent pool, increased productivity, and cost savings related to reduced office space and overheads.

Ultimately, success in distributed teams comes down to clear communication, trust, and a commitment to delivering results. By setting expectations early and maintaining open lines of communication, both team members and managers can thrive in this dynamic and increasingly prevalent work environment.

Here's how we do it

Remote Team Connect is designed specifically to help businesses source and secure top-tier offshore talent at lightning speed and lower cost than any other system currently available.

Precision targeting: We use advanced targeting tools to place your job ads in front of the right candidates based on skills, experience, and industry relevance. This includes databases we have carefully curated from having run hundreds of campaigns for clients across diverse roles and countries.

Engaging copy: Our job ads are crafted to stand out, highlighting the key benefits of working with your company and the potential for growth and impact.

Disqualifying process: We ensure your candidates share the right information, allowing us to disqualify those who do not meet your criteria. We aim to get you high-quality candidates, saving you time sifting through the resumes of those who are not a fit.

Intelligent AI: Our AI-driven matching process sifts and sorts the candidates, eliminating hundreds at lightning speed.

Analytics and optimisation: We ensure your openings get noticed by top talent by continuously monitoring the performance of our ads and tweaking them for maximum reach and engagement.

You are not just posting a job; you are strategically positioning your company in a global talent market, ready to attract the leaders of tomorrow.

Our fixed-fee, all-inclusive service includes:

- Suggested salary and payment process for your new team members
- Professional copywriting of your job ad
- Placement of your ad on our vast networks and on LinkedIn
- Video recording and transcripts of candidates answering your qualifying questions
- Assessment of candidates' resumes and video interviews
- Assessment of experience, skill proficiency, and industry knowledge
- Personality profile – an outline of the candidate's potential for success and fit within your team
- DISC Profile – a ranking score for Dominance, Influence, Steadiness and Conscientiousness
- All candidates are ranked against each other to give you your priority list for one-to-one interviews
- A minimum of 20 qualifying candidates to choose from
- Onboarding guideline
- Pro forma contract for your hires

Video recording candidates

View candidates' responses to key questions before the interview stage to save time, reduce bias, and make more informed decisions. This ensures you get a genuine feel for each candidate's communication skills, personality, and suitability for the role.

Candidate assessment

Our expert team meticulously evaluates each resume and video interview, providing you with a comprehensive analysis of each candidate's qualifications, skills, and cultural fit.

Your top 10 candidates

By combining expert resume assessments and insightful video interviews, we meticulously evaluate and filter candidates to present you with the top 10 most qualified and suitable individuals.

Receive a shortlist of the best-suited candidates, ready for your final review.

If you'd like to organise a time to speak with our team further, review this page and reach out to us today for an obligation-free chat about what might be possible for you.

https://www.prominence.global/remote-teams

Acknowledgements

Writing a book is often seen as the work of the author and it is we who usually receive all of the accolades. A well known saying I'm sure you've heard is: "It takes a village to raise a child".

Equally, it takes a team to write a book. I'm truly proud of The Distributed Teams Playbook you are reading today, as with all previous titles, I put my heart and soul into my part in creating it for you.

However, my heart felt gratitude goes to:

David Dugan, my business partner, mentor and friend. It was he who encouraged and motivated me to write this one. Additionally, he has been silently by my side over the last ten amazing years, guiding and expanding on the incredible business we built together from an idea, into the multi award winning and globally recognised version it is today.

Dixie Maria Carlton, my publishing specialist. Dixie and her amazing team at Indie Experts have been part of this book from the day I committed to writing it. They are the ones who take an idea to a first draft manuscript, then turn it into something I can be proud to put my name to. From mentorship, editing, stretching my thinking, cover design, layout and of course publishing, they play a huge role in the entire book writing journey.

The Prominence team, all of you across the globe have been aware of the journey from the start to write this book. I can't thank you enough for creating the space for me to put the time and energy into this process. Additionally, they are the inspiration behind the book. Together, we built a business a little differently that works incredibly well.

And, finally. To my amazing wife Julie, she is my rock. Another well-known saying you'd know "behind every successful man stands a great women". It's certainly true in my case. She is there for me through every challenge, every win and every trip around the country or across the globe.

This is my team and village.

About Adam Houlahan

Adam Houlahan is a renowned LinkedIn expert and member of the prestigious Top Voice program, making him one of only a handful of LinkedIn specialist to be recognised for his expertise by LinkedIn. He's a best-selling author, and international keynote speaker. Known for his powerful influence strategies and deep understanding of LinkedIn's unique social dynamics, Adam has empowered thousands of entrepreneurs and business leaders to elevate their personal brands and drive impactful growth through social media. His notable works, including **Social Media Secret Sauce**, **The LinkedIn Playbook**, and **Influencer**, have set the standard for ethical, results-driven LinkedIn strategies, showcasing his commitment to fostering authentic connections and meaningful engagement.

As CEO of Prominence Global, one of the world's leading LinkedIn agency for entrepreneurs, Adam spearheads innovative approaches that help clients harness the full potential of LinkedIn. He's helped create over 12 million impacts in global giving projects, reflecting his dedication not only to business growth but also to global social impact. Adam's work emphasises a structured, practical approach to influence, built on trust and authentic leadership—values he brings to every keynote, training, and consulting engagement.

Adam's expertise has made him a sought-after speaker and educator, sharing actionable insights on how to cultivate influence, connect with ideal clients, and stand out in today's digital world. Through Prominence Global, he continues to shape the future of LinkedIn marketing, empowering individuals to expand their reach, establish authority, and lead with purpose.

▼

Testimonials

This is a Beautiful Blueprint (actually a Bible) not just for scaling but for running and building a Brilliant Business from Day One (or wherever your business is right now).

The level of detail here is stunning. It goes beyond classics like the E-Myth and pours on layer after layer of 'how-to's' that are absolutely stand out.

And Adam doesn't just write about it — he lives this book every day.

And he brings that feeling directly to you on every page.

Destined to be a classic — get it and do it as soon as you can.

— PAUL DUNN

Co-Founder B1G1 | B1G1.com

Building a high-performing distributed team in multiple time zones takes more finesse than simply calling up your local recruitment agency.

Adam shows how to build powerful working connections that transcend borders - because great teams aren't bound by geography, only by vision, trust and empowerment.

A must-read for business leaders who want to grow globally and reduce their labour costs by leveraging high-calibre offshore talent.

— GAVIN LISTER

Lister Consulting | gavinlister.com

I hired my first remote worker in 2007. In 2016 we got rid of our office and focused on hiring the best people for the money, rather than those who happened to live in the same city as ours.

Today all my companies are 'global first' meaning our customers and our team are distributed around the world.

It took me many years and countless, expensive, mistakes to figure out how to do this well.

'The Distributed Teams Blueprint' will save you a fortune and can even teach those of us who have been doing it for years some new tricks. Highly recommend this book!

— CALLUM LAING

Entrepreneur/Investor/Author | CallumLaing.com

Finally, a real-world, practical guide on how to scale results using remote teams. So many books on this subject have proven to be theoretically interesting but practically ineffective.

Like the author, I've run remote teams (currently across 7 countries and all in different time zones) and I wish to heck I'd had this book 15 years ago.

In fact, it's more of a guide book than a traditional book because it gives you proven, practical processes and protocols for scaling your results by looking after your team and supporting them, and at the same time demonstrating care for them and their loved ones.

My favourite part is The Buddy System because it acknowledges the power of diverse perspectives and demonstrates trust in Team Members.

— TOM POLAND

www.Leadsology.guru

I have certainly had my share of VA's in the past, and made more than my fair share of mistakes. I wish this book had been written a couple of years ago. It would have saved me a lot of money and lost productivity.

Adam's book has given me some great insights on how to get the best out of, and improve the productivity of my remote team, improve the connection with our local team and create a much more streamlined system of onboarding future team members.

Highly recommend this book if you are looking to grow and scale your business using the amazing abundance of talent that exists abroad.

Would give it 6 stars if I could.

— KARL SCHWANTES

Founder of Reputable | Reputable.com
Author of Rock Her World

A comprehensive, easy to read and easy to implement roadmap to successfully build your own distributed team. From sourcing candidates, to selection, to contract negotiations, to onboarding, to communications, to managing your targeted and talented team of experts - this book is your one stop shop.

— KATE CHRISTIE

Time management expert
Best selling author of The Life List

Think of this book as your step by step guide into the uncharted territory of distributed teams, pointing the way to seamless integration, innovation and performance. Adam's book is full of simple steps and processes to help you hire, induct, lead and get the absolute best outcome from an overseas team.

— ROGER SIMPSON

CEO, The Retail Solution
Author of The Ultimate Retail Sales Experience

Think of your team as the modern orchestra of business - each member playing their part harmoniously. This is especially true for distributed teams where each member, no matter how distant, adds their contribution to create a symphony of success.

Adam Houlahan doesn't just conduct, he hands you the sheet music, step-by-step, so your team can play with precision, alignment and excellence. This book isn't really about remote work - it's a master blueprint for building resilient, thriving teams that redefine what's possible in a hyper-connected, global marketplace.

— SIMON BOWEN

Founder The Models Method ©
Creator The Genius Model ©

Adam is exceptional at taking the complex and making it simple and easy to digest.

This book is the 'cheat sheet' to creating effective and aligned teams in a global economy.

All leaders can utilise this resource to tun their remote workforce into their greatest competitive advantage.

— CHANDELL LABBOZZETTA

Author, Confident Closing

Distributed teams are part of the future, but leading distributed teams isn't easy. Adam's focus on the most important blocks of true team success helps navigate a huge challenge, and even bigger opportunity.

— BEN NASH

Author of Get Unstuck, Replace Your Salary By Investing, Virgin Millionaire

As a full-time digital nomad, I realise the power and benefits of building a remote team, which allows you to hire based on skill sets instead of traditional geographical limits. Adam covers all the hurdles you might find and, most importantly, gives you a proven process to ensure success in building and leveraging a remote team.

— WAYNE SCHMIDT

Former country manager Xero
Current Digital Nomad

Having spent considerable time leading a global remote organisation, I find this book to be an exceptional resource that addresses the real challenges executives face today. Unlike many leadership texts that remain in the theoretical realm, this comprehensive guide delivers actionable insights for managing distributed teams.

What sets this book apart is its granular approach to remote leadership. It methodically walks through each phase of remote team management, offering concrete solutions rather than platitudes. From establishing virtual communication protocols to maintaining culture across time zones, the guidance is rooted in practical application.

As CEOs, we need frameworks that translate directly to our complex operating environments. This book stands out by addressing the nuanced challenges that aren't covered in traditional management literature - the very issues that keep us up at night when leading remote teams. Whether you're transitioning to a remote model or optimizing an existing distributed workforce, the step-by-step methodology provides clear direction for implementation.

I particularly appreciate how the content aligns with the realities of modern executive leadership. It's a valuable playbook that will serve as a go-to reference for any leader serious about building and scaling high-performing remote teams.

— DR. ANDRÉE BATES

CEO & Founder of Eularis

Adam is the real deal, giving easy-to-follow guidance so you can survive and thrive with global teams.

— COLIN HUNT,

Founder ezygrowth.world

In this book, Adam Houlahan offers the essential strategies necessary to successfully managing a global remote workforce. From navigating time zones and cultural differences to leveraging overlooked talent pools, this guide offers fresh, practical insights to help your business thrive in the modern era of distributed teams.

— JOHN RAY

Managing Partner, John Ray Co.
Author, The Generosity Mindset

.

www.ingramcontent.com/pod-product-compliance
Lightning Source LLC
Chambersburg PA
CBHW041259040426
42334CB00028BA/3087